ISRAEL
BASICS

What every Christian should know

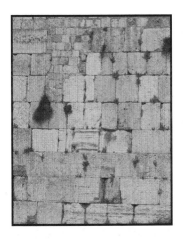

K. J. FROLANDER

ISBN 978-0-692-01440-0

Acknowledgements

Thank you to Yahweh without whom none of us, nor the material or events recorded here would have existed. You truly are an amazing and loving God. Who can search you out and know all Your ways? I love that you let me try!

Thank you to my parents who have believed in me from the beginning and supported me and this writing/teaching project to its completion.

Thank you to Diane Withers whose Israel 101 small group first opened my eyes to "this Israel stuff" and the Jewish People who are held so dearly in God's heart.

Thank you to Christian Friends of Israel who gave me the opportunity in 2007 & 2008 to volunteer, live in the land, and interact with hundreds of Israelis on a monthly basis and become acquainted with modern Israeli culture.

And thank you to all my dear Jerusalem friends who afforded me so many wonderful experiences in Israel, the coffees, the chats, the walks, the crazy taxi rides, the road trips around the country, all getting to know the Land and the special People whom God loves and has set apart.

Israel Basics: What every Christian should know

An easy-to-use, small group format
for the history, culture and prophecy of Israel

Table of Contents

Author's note

For this second edition I would like to explain why I've changed my use of BCE and CE to the original abbreviations of BC and AD. Most scholarly writings today use Before Common Era (BCE) and Common Era (CE) to distinguish time and we have been told this is the modern and scientific representation of time, but in changing the distinction of "Before Christ" (BC) to "Before Common Era" modernity has tried to erase the central point of when history became the Common Era: Jesus. Jesus coming to redeem mankind changed everything, including the way we keep time. Therefore in acknowledgement of His birth and sacrifice, I am using Before Christ (BC) and *Anno Domini* (AD) which translated from the Latin means "In the Year of our Lord." Long live the King!

INTRODUCTION AND OVERVIEW

Before the beginning, God had an ultimate plan. This grand and divine design He has been orchestrating through individuals' ordinary decisions and through the nations in their collective decisions. If everything were written, it would be a (hi)story too massive for any one human being to understand in his lifetime. There are all kinds of filters people use to break history into a grid that traces mankind's progress over time. Communism, Secularism, Humanism, Buddhism, Christianity, Islam and hundreds more, each produce their own unique emphasis on historical events. The grid an individual chooses is called his "worldview."

A biblical worldview processes the story of humankind through this grid[1.1]: There is a God. He is pure. He made everything, for His own purposes and enjoyment. He set up the rules and then made mankind. Sin entered the world through man, yet God wanted reconciled relationship with man. So He chose a man (Abraham) from among men to be a light to the nations. God grew Abraham into a nation (Israel) to shine light into the world.

Because they were chosen to shine light into the world, Israel was given a code of conduct (Torah). The Torah set up the Jewish people to be successful in all they do, *if* they follow the commands. They will be blessed with abundance, they won't get sick, they will multiply, they will be full of peace and joy. The Torah is not a rigid set of rules that are burdensome. It is the plan of God to prosper a people, to set them apart. The Torah was designed to elevate a people to live fully alive, connected to God as a representation of Him. The nations were to have seen a prospering nation of people and been provoked to jealously ask, "What is it that makes life work for you?" and the Jew was to smile and say, "Come and meet my God!" thus, bringing the nations in repentance back to reconciliation in the heart of the Living God.

The Jews were chosen to be a light to the world. Not that one nation was better than another, it was a choice. His choice. God's ultimate plan continues to unfold daily in human choices and events. It is very easy to follow the threads of the plan when they appear written down and explained in the Bible, but it is a little more difficult today. For example: Assyria. God used this wicked nation as a rod of His anger to punish

Israel and other nations for their sins. But Assyria went too far and God had to punish them through the Babylonians.

So how do we know what God is doing now? It is more difficult to see any pattern when you are in the midst of it, but think about this modern example Rabbi Jamie Cowen explains[1.1]: Before the first Iraq War, it looked like Saddam Hussein devised a plan to capture all the oil fields of Kuwait. But what most people don't realize is that Kuwait was the primary source of funding for the Palestinian Liberation Organization (PLO), which was constantly attacking Israel. When Kuwait was being destroyed by Hussein, they no longer sent money to the PLO. The PLO's lack of funding is what caused Yasser Arafat (leader of PLO) to seek peace with Israel. Everything looked like it was going fine with Saddam Hussein, then he made a critical error in judgment. He went too far. Hussein began to send rockets over Israel's borders himself! Just like the Assyrians went too far and God destroyed them, Hussein's army was destroyed. He soon lost the war, and within years he and his sons were living in holes in the ground. The sons lost their lives, and he is currently in American prison, all power, palaces and pretention stripped away.

What a privilege it is for us living in this day and age who have eyes of the heart to see. We get to watch the unfolding of God's plan on the evening news! In these perilous last days it is more imperative than ever to understand God's heart and live our lives in agreement with God's heart. It is not as terribly complicated as we try to make it though.

Here's what we know: 1. God is at work in human history. He has a plan for the salvation of the nations. 2. God will use the Jewish people to affect all the nations (Gen 22:18). 3. Ultimately all the nations will come worship the LORD in Jerusalem (Jer 3:17).

Everything happening in the world today and in history is a part of the Ultimate Plan. Understanding the plan of God through Jewish history, and as it is unfolding, will offer Christian hearts the proper grid with which to process world events. It will encourage Christians to jump on-board with God's plan and bless the Jewish people so they can do the job God created for them from the foundation of the earth: be the light to the nations, drawing them back to their Creator.

CULTURE VS RELIGION

It can get tricky when trying to understand the Jewish people as an outsider (non-Jewish, Gentile or *Goyim*). Because of their unique history (which will we get to dig into), "Jewish" refers to both a religion and a culture. The two are so intertwined it is difficult to see them separately. Most of the things the average American Christian associates with being Jewish are actually cultural or traditional, rather than religious. Though, the original religion is what has generally dictated Jewish culture. This culture comes from both times the Jews were exiled from Israel (as a punishment for sin) they needed to form a way of keeping the Torah outside the borders of their country, while functioning under new secular governments. This keeping of Torah, a submission to the God of Abraham, Isaac and Jacob, is what makes a person Jewish. In foreign lands, it definitely made the Jews stand out. It brought them success occasionally, and was more than difficult at other times. For many millions of Jews, being followers of the Torah brought death. Very unpleasant death.

A decision that will influence whether or not you fulfill your complete destiny is this: Where do you stand with Israel? Every believer is called to bless Israel!

God says, "I will bless those who bless you, and I will curse those who curse you," (Gen 12:3) speaking to Israel. Every civilization who has blessed the Jewish people has prospered, until they turned away from the

> Where you stand with Israel could determine whether you fulfill your complete destiny!

Jewish people. Every time a civilization or faction of a civilization or leaders of nations have sought to harm the Jewish people, they have lost their power and influence, no matter how strong or un-topple-able they once were. (The ancient Egyptians, the ancient Persians, the Romans, the Spanish, the Ottomans, the British).

In these last days, as the nations gather against Israel (as promised in Zech 12:3 that the whole world will oppose Israel), it is going to be harder and harder for us to stand with Israel and bless her as the Lord Jesus desires us to do. However, it is imperative that we as the Christian

Church do just that! Even if it costs us our lives. Our destiny depends on it.

Revelation 12:11 says we overcome the enemy by the blood of the Lamb and the word of our testimony. The "blood of the Lamb" has already been accomplished through Jesus' death on the cross and resurrection from the dead. It is the "word of our testimony" that we are working on.

Testimonies are so valuable. We allow others to see into our hearts, the inner-me, by sharing our testimony. Yes, a testimony glorifies God, His power, His love and care for people, and testimony encourages others to trust that Jesus cares for them the same way. But it is more than that. The word of our testimony exposes, and gives lift and oxygen, buoyancy to the love that God has for the inner-me of each of us, and it passes that God-kind of love on to the human hearts of the hearer of testimonies.

Have you noticed that when you hear someone's story, their struggles, their triumphs, their dreams that you feel closer to them? You are gaining an affinity that is inherent to the human story of life. Even our structure of law systems allows both sides of a story to be heard before a judgment is pronounced. It is testimony. The power of testimony must be another one of those God-mysteries He is so good at.

This book is a testimony of Israel, of sorts, so that you can gain an inherent love and affinity for Israel, by knowing her story. There are so many lessons and parts of God that we can know by studying Israel and how God relates to her and deals with her, that we might not otherwise know.

Israel is the apple of God's eye (Duet 32:10, Zech 2:8). It means that she is ever before Him, and constantly on His heart.

But why Israel? Why the Jews? (They often wonder the same thing. The character of Tevye asks this iconic question in the movie *Fiddler on the Roof*[1], "...once in a while, couldn't You choose someone else?")

The short answer is that yes, God could have chosen some other group, some other land, but Israel is His choice.

Israel is not a "back up plan" because the Flood of Noah's day did not work. After mankind chose sin in the Garden of Eden, God's plan of Redemption was activated. Adam and Eve's walks in the cool of the day, living before a holy God, naked and unashamed, the sharing of hearts and love in relationship have always been God's purpose for man. Man was created by God for relationship with God. Man's inner-me was shaped and formed with loving fingers to feel fulfillment and perfection and rightness when in relationship with the God Who made him.

Somewhere along the line of time we lost sight of what it means and feels like to live in right relationship with the God who created us. Probably that first evening after Adam and Eve were ejected from the Garden of perfection, they missed their walk with the Lord, and began "the forgetting" in which mankind dwells today. God fore-knew that this would happen. He knew that one day, in this generation, He would give you life, and you would not remember what it is like to live in perfect relationship and love with a holy God. He knew that you would not remember Who He is, and so, He created and chose a people called Israel. Israel would be a people set apart from all other people. They would be a living object lesson for mankind. God wanted to remind mankind of the perfect relationship they could be enjoying with Him. Israel would forever be a reminder of the purity of God, the set-apartness of God, the faithfulness of God, the wholly-unlike-any-other-ness of God.

Into the culture of this people Israel, He would place markers and reminders (called the Feasts of the Lord) to teach mankind of Himself. He would place ordinary men into this culture, exposing their strengths and weaknesses for all to see, so that they would become guides to pattern our hearts after. We call them "heroes of the faith;" God called them by name and counts them as friends.

With few exceptions, they were all Jews. And in case you've not fully come to terms with it: Jesus was Jewish. He was not Catholic, or Presbyterian, or Baptist or Charismatic. He wasn't even non-denominational. He was Jewish.

Christianity makes much more sense when lived within the framework of Jesus being a Jewish man when He taught the Beatitudes, when He

11

cleansed the Temple, when He died on the cross. Judaism today contains many traditions of men, good men trying to please God, but men just the same. Identifying which traditions are manmade and which are the statutes of God can only be accomplished through studying the Scripture God gave (the Torah) and the history of the people He chose to express Himself to mankind through.

As we study these lessons it is important to keep two things in mind.
1. Israel's testimony is not yet complete. While they are our example, they are also in need of redemption.
2. Israel's story is a love story. It is a wooing of a people's heart to the One Who loves them more than life itself. One Whose goal is eternity with His Beloved, and Who is willing to risk short term hardship to bring her heart to Him forever. He sees the end from the beginning.

These lessons will unravel mysteries and fill in key puzzle pieces that you may not have even realized were missing. Read the Scripture as a love letter to a bride, designed to show love and set a people apart from the rest of mankind, not as a set of rules that dare not be broken.

Jesus did not come to "set us free" from the Law, but to fulfill it. His words, not mine! (Matt 5:17).

Many in the American Church have pre-conceived notions about the Jewish people that are just wrong, or they may not have any knowledge at all. Our hearts don't seem to connect with the fact that the Israelites of Exodus and Ruth are the same people as the Israelis we greet in the mall kiosk selling Dead Sea mud or represented on the evening news lamenting the loss of a loved one in yet another bombing or rocket attack in Israel.

Israel has been through much torment in her history. But, the enemy of Israel is not the Arabs, or Muslims, or ignorant Christians, or atheists, or you insert your 'favorite' anti-Semitic group here. The hatred goes back way farther than that, before even the Garden of Eden, to a fateful decision in heaven made by that beautiful archangel and worship leader, Lucifer. We won't go into a theology of how the sins of pride and attempting to steal (worship) were allowed in heaven. That is a whole other book. It is sufficient to say, he did (Is. 14:12-14) and thus God became Lucifer's enemy. Not in any kind of equality of hero/arch-enemy—If anything, Satan would be on par with the angels Michael and Gabriel—but Lucifer/Satan set himself against God. He sets himself in place to try to lure what belongs to God to himself. Tries.

Because God set Israel apart for Himself and to reveal Himself to mankind, Satan tries to destroy Israel, and make God a liar. Never going to happen! But Satan will use whatever means he has available to take what belongs to God. It is imperative to separate in our minds the enemy of Israel (Satan) from the tools he is currently using (Islam, terrorists and ignorance). Formerly, Satan used Christians in Crusades!

Anti-Semitism is choosing to align oneself against the chosen people of God, Jews/Israel. Christians cannot have any part of it, and yet, it runs rampant in the Church at large! In this instance in makes no difference who the people actually are, the bottom line is that one is choosing to persecute (or ignore!) the apple of God's eye.

The following sections of this introduction are designed to unlock some of the Jewish mysteriousness for American Christians who have always wondered, "what's *that* about?" when they have seen modern Judaism.

A Little Background to Modern Jewish Culture:
The Shma—Duet 6:4-9 This is the most important prayer of the Hebrew faith. They sing/say it at the beginning of every corporate meeting. The Christians in the Land of Israel have adopted its use as well. The following scripture is the basis of Judaism

Hear, O Israel: The LORD our God, the LORD is one.
Love the LORD your God with all your heart and with all your soul and with all your strength. These commandments that I give you today are to be upon your hearts. Impress them on your children. Talk about them when you sit at home and when you walk along the road, when you lie down and when you get up. Tie

---

Try singing it:
Shma, Yisrael, Adonai Elo-hay-nu, Adonai Echad. Baruch shem kavod, malchuto, le-olam, va'ed

---

13

them as symbols on your hands and bind them on your foreheads. Write them on the doorframes of your houses and on your gates.

This scripture is a part of a Jew's everyday life: The children are constantly involved in the reading of scripture, and they have specific parts to play in holy holiday celebrations. During all Shabbat (Saturday rest day) celebrations and holidays, religious families sit around and speak of the miracles of the Bible and the commands. They read their weekly Torah Portion (similar to a One-Year Bible, except broken into weekly instead of daily portions) at home, on the bus and when waiting in line (although "line" is not exactly the term Americans would use!). During official prayer times, (mornings only) the men tie a leather strap around their non-dominate arm called *tefillin*, and they strap a little box of scriptures to their foreheads called "head tefillin" or "phylacteries." They wear a prayer shawl called a *tallit* to 1.) show their submission God's authority, 2.) be "under His covering." (It makes a nice tent of privacy for praying too!) and 3.) fulfill the Numb 15:38-40 which commands that *"They shall make themselves tzitzit on the corners of their garments throughout their generations, and they shall place on the tzitzit of each corner a thread of techeilet. And it shall be tzitzit for you, and you will see it, and you will remember all the mitzvot of the L-RD and do them and not follow your heart or your eyes and run after them.* They wear this during ALL prayer times.

Also under or over their clothing the devout men wear a poncho-like small *tallit* all the time and usually leave the *tzitzit* strings hanging out to show their devotion to God and to His Law. "There is a complex procedure for tying the knots of the *tzitzit*, filled with religious and numerological significance."[1] These are the strings you might have seen hanging out of a Jewish man's shirt tails.

This is the prayer[2] they recite as they wrap the *tefillin* around their fingers translated into English:

> I will betroth you to me forever
> Betroth you to me in righteousness,
> in justice, and in kindness and in mercy
> I will betroth you to me in faithfulness and
> you will know the Lord.

What's that thing they put on the door? A *Mezuzah*

Every doorway in Israel has a little scroll-shaped box containing verses of scripture called a *mezuzah* (meaning from the Hebrew: "doorpost") screwed into the door frame. Even shops have this at their doorframe. Devout Jews will touch the *mezuzah* and kiss their fingers and upon entry and exit to show their reverence for God.

Rich[2] expresses it this way, "Every time you pass through a door with a *mezuzah* on it, you touch the *mezuzah* and then kiss the fingers that touched it, expressing love and respect for G-d...

> "It is proper to remove a mezuzah when you move, and in fact, it is usually recommended. If you leave it in place, the subsequent owner may treat it with disrespect, and this is a grave sin. I have seen many mezuzot in apartment complexes that have been painted over because a subsequent owner failed to remove it while the building was painted, and it breaks my heart every time I see that sort of disrespect to an object of religious significance."[2]

Also, the name of God is so holy, that they do not dare to utter it aloud, nor even write it. So Jews would write in English "G-d" and they call God, *Ha Shem* meaning "the name." The Jews have a very clear understanding of God's purity and our unworthiness.

We as Christians are blessed because we have accepted the holy blood of Jesus to cover us, and by that, we are seen by God as untainted, so that we can enter into relationship with Him. We can enjoy speaking and writing His name, and the power that is contained within the name of Jesus and the Names of God (which is a WHOLE other study!).

CHAPTER 1
LESSON: THE MIRACLE OF MODERN ISRAEL IN OVERVIEW

Teacher notes: Every class will need Bibles available to read from. In the first meeting, reviewing the introduction will help set people's hearts to properly engage with these lessons on Israel. Topics: Intro—overview of class, maps, ancient and modern. There will be much reading in this class. Read scriptures that promised the curse of dispersion and then restoration after the Diaspora and the modern fulfillment.

Introduction
The story of Israel is a love story. God Almighty is the Lover, and the Lady of Israel is the Beloved. Many times throughout scripture this analogy is evident from the Psalms, Song of Solomon (implied throughout), Hosea (his whole ministry), Isaiah (61:10, 62:5), Jeremiah (2:2), and in the New Testament, all four Gospels & Revelation. God's longing for his bride is a common Biblical theme. So as we study the ups and downs of the history of the Beloved, Israel, keep in mind the passion a bridegroom has for his bride, because even though God also implicates Himself as a father, it is His passion as a bridegroom that causes Him to always pursue Israel.

Can a nation be born in a day? (Isaiah 66:8)
The current nation of Israel declared its independence and was recognized as a new nation by the United Nations on May 14, 1948. But the nation of Israel (the people) was recognized and prophesied to return to the Land of their origins as long ago as 792 to 915 BC, (Isaiah 49: 8-23). After 1,875 years in exile, assimilation, persecution and fleeing and assimilation, persecution and fleeing... it is a wonder and a miracle that God reestablished this nation state in the very real estate that He chose with Abraham back in the 17th century BC!! It shows God's character of faithfulness. When He says He will do something, we can count on it, even 3,600 years later.

Exiles Overview
Three times Israel has been exiled from the land (living outside the borders God gave them). The first was when they went to Egypt with

Joseph as a fledgling nation, when they were more of a tribe or band than a nation, around 1700 BC, where Israel lived for 400 years and became enslaved before Moses rose up as their deliverer in the 13th century BC.

The second time was a little more complex in that Israel had split into two kingdoms. The northern kingdom was called Israel and the southern kingdom, including Jerusalem, was called Judah. They each had their own line of kings. The northern kingdom of Israel was conquered by the Assyrians in 722 to 720 BC, and Judah (the remaining people) was conquered by the Babylonians in 586 BC.

The third (and hopefully final) exile is commonly called the Diaspora. And it was "the big one!" It began in 70 AD, about 45 years after Jesus died and rose to life again. The Romans had been occupying Israel for many years, but well and truly conquered them and laid waste to Israel and Jerusalem and the second Temple (we will talk all about the temples at a later date), the final holdouts were holed up in Herod's defensible compound in the Judean Wilderness called Masada, which again, is a great story that we will cover in detail in the coming lessons. The final assault ended in 73 AD, and those people of God that still remained alive were for the most part scattered across Rome and *Dura Europos* (near Euphrates River).[3] As these kingdoms/nations were conquered by other rulers, the Jews scattered farther and farther until they were sprinkled all over the current Middle East and Europe. They were concentrated in Turkey, Italy, northern Africa, southern France, and southern Spain.

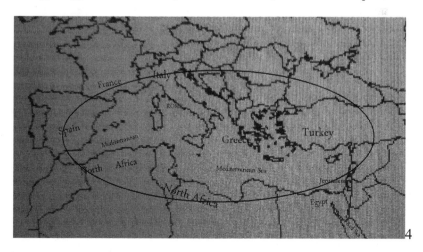

Diaspora: Centuries of loathing in Europe Overview

Well, after being dispersed it only got worse through the centuries for the Jewish people. Yes, there were some times of rest, but mostly it has been almost 2,000 years of persecution and loathing. The webpage http://www.simpletoremember.com/articles/a/HistoryJewishPersecution/ shows an overview of these persecutions such as in the 600's in Spain and Europe the Jews were forced to convert to Christianity; in the 800's they were expelled from Italy, made slaves and their property was confiscated.

In the 1000's there were massacres and LIVE burnings in Spain, France, Rome, Hungary, Jerusalem and other nations which no longer exist. In the 1100's there were pogroms in Kiev (Russia) and massacres all over modern day Germany. In England, Jewish property was confiscated. The 1200's were particularly bad as Jews were expelled from their homes almost everywhere from England east to Spain, Austria, Rome, and they were forced to wear the "red badge of shame," or a pointed dunce hat (Austria). There were public hangings, all rights as citizens were revoked, and the Inquisition was instituted in Rome. This was during the times of the Crusades.[5] This brutality was executed by people claiming to be Christians, and done in the name of God to avenge Jesus' death.

It only got worse in the 1300's especially in Spain, and by 1492, the Spanish Inquisition began for those Jews who were left or who had returned. The Spanish Inquisition was one of the worst times of torture in history, and all done in the name of God! The 1500's offered no rest for God's people. In Berlin in 1510, Jews were publically tortured and executed. They were systematically expelled from the following nations/cities in the 1500's: Strasburg, Regensburg, Cracow, Naples, Bohemia, Genoa, Bavaria, Pesaro, Poland, Austria, Prague, Wurzburg, the Papel States, Brandanburg, Netherlands, Brunswick, Cremona, Pavia and Lodi. Portugal had stake burnings. Then in 1615 it began to happen in earnest all over Germany.[5]

The 1700's and 1800's brought no rest and the Jews were expelled from Russia, Lithuania, Bordeaux, Austria, Prussia, even the Russian countryside. In 1768, 3,000 Jews were slaughtered in Kiev.[5]

The 1900's brought humanity her greatest shame. In the first 40 years of the 1900's, we tortured Jews all over Europe culminated in murdering 6 MILLION (formerly-Israelite) men, women and children. That many zeros cannot even find a place of comprehension in my brain: at 2 seconds per person, it would take about 139 DAYS to count them all. Two-thirds of the earth's population of God's chosen people were wiped out!

WHY? How does this string of information come into any sort of order or sense? Where is the reason? Where is justice? How did this happen? How does this KEEP happening to this same group of people?

Before the Beginning Overview
To understand as much as we are able to on this side of eternity we will have to go back, way back to before the beginning. Here is a short little play by play:

God was. And He had His angels around worshipping Him in His splendor as was right and proper, and Lucifer, the "worship leader" decides that he wants God's worship and His place for himself. So he stages a coup, and 1/3 of the angels follow him. (Doesn't go so well, God being God and all-knowing and all!) Lucifer and his cohorts get kicked out of heaven and they are now called Satan and demons in the current vernacular.

Then in the Beginning, God created heaven and Earth…and plants and animals each with the male and female counterparts. Then, He created mankind, fashioned in His own image, as His own counterpart, and He placed them in the pristine Garden of Eden with one Law: Do not eat of the fruit of the Tree of Knowledge of Good and Evil. And they were able to talk and walk with the Almighty face to face, worshipping Him and being loved by Him purely!

Soon, Satan sees another way to usurp God's Glory for himself. He invites Adam and Eve to break the one Law, and they do. Bad News! Now they are separated from God by sin. God is heartbroken but not stumped. He (already) has a plan to reconcile man to Himself.

So, mankind continues in his own way, each generation falling farther from God, becoming more entrapped in sin. Finally after 2,256 years (arrived at by adding the ages of the generations of Noah listed in Genesis) after creation, or about 3536 BC[6] God sends a Flood to wipe out the sin and start over with Noah's family. (Noah's sons were Ham, Shem, and Japheth).

Mankind begins to re-populate the earth, but sin is still here. And God is still yearning for a counterpart to Himself, as He has given all the other things He created, one with whom He can commune. But it is just not happening. Mankind with our fallen nature does not withstand Satan's temptations to choose our own way instead of God's way. Finally, after 1,330 more years (c.2200 BC), God finds a man—an idol maker of all people—who has the guts to respond "yes" to His call to come away to a new place out of Ur of the Chaldeans. His name was Abram, and he was from the line Noah's son Shem (from whose name we take the word "Semite"). And God makes a covenant with Abram to form a new race of people who will be dedicated to their Creator.[6] The first couple of generations (Isaac & Jacob) were a mess, yet they tried to follow God and the covenant He had made with Abraham (name change).

In the 3rd & 4th generation the clan of Hebrews numbered about 70 people. When God allowed famine in Canaan, they all moved to Egypt where God in His all-knowing-ness had sent Joseph (4th generation) ahead to rule and help save the known-world from starving to death. After a while in Egypt, the Pharaohs became afraid of the rapidly expanding population of Hebrews and enslaved them. For 400 years they worked. Little is known about the religious state of the Hebrews during this time, but something set them apart, or the Egyptians would not have feared them. The work strengthened their bodies, and helped meld them together as a nation, set apart. After God showed His power to set the Hebrews free of the Egyptian enslavement (The 10 Plagues, Moses, and the Parting of the Red Sea events) the Hebrews still had trouble fully dedicating themselves to Him as the *only* God, as seen during the whole Golden Calf event. Ironically, Moses was on Mt Sinai receiving the Ten Commandments when this idol worship was going on. The Ten Commandments then became 613 laws (248 positive, 365 negative). Blessings and cursings would follow those who entered into this Covenant with God depending on whether the people kept their side of the covenant or not. God was always faithful. They did not *have* to enter this covenant, they chose to. This covenant was an opportunity to be reunited with their Creator which had been impossible since sin entered into the world. Once they chose God, they became *His* people forever, and the enemy of God set himself against them too. Satan is always trying to lure their hearts away from God through fear and intimidation and through stirring up their desire to worship anything other than God.

As the Hebrew nation began to conquer the Promised Land that God had pointed out to Abraham 500 years or so before, they dealt with fear, and, unfortunately, gave into it a lot. But not always! As they wandered in the desert and later possessed the Promised Land, they became the nation of Israel—who spoke "Hebrew." For generations and generations Israel would worship God and then fall into sin. God would let it go for a while, calling them to repentance (which rarely happened as recorded in Scripture), then He would send prophets to warn them of what would happen—usually skirmishes or all-out wars. Then they would turn back to God. It would last for a little while, sometimes not even a full generation, and they would slip back into the same idol worship as the pagan nations that surrounded them indulged in. Now "idol worship" doesn't sound so horrible, but these false gods (ultimately Satan) required sacrifice and worship. Some people even burned their own infants/children in the fire to appease these "idols." And that is pure evil!

Then Israel wanted their own king like all the other nations, not some God they couldn't see ruling them. This came about around 1020 BC. This bright idea lasted through three generations of kings: Saul, David and Solomon. Then the nation of Israel was torn into two kingdoms, Israel and Judah in 930 BC.

By 722 BC, the stink of sin had become intolerable to God, and He moved the Assyrian Army in to conquer the northern kingdom of Israel. They were taken captive. Judah, the southern kingdom, remained in the cycle of sin, warning, repentance, restoration, sin, warning, repentance, restoration...for another 134 years until 586 BC when the Babylonians conquered them. Judah was carried away into captivity. Jeremiah prophesied that it would last 70 years, (during the lifetimes of Daniel, Shadrach, Meshack and Abed-Nego, Queen Esther, Nehemiah and Ezra), and then the Hebrews were given freedom to return. (It was during this time of Isaiah, Jeremiah and Ezekiel that God's idea of a personal Messiah first is recorded prophetically in the writings that became Scripture.) A first delegation returned to the land of Israel from captivity followed by a second 100 years later. But Israel was never quite the same. There were no more kings of Israel, though there was a restored priesthood and a restored temple by 515 BC. (This is called the Second Temple period.) Then Israel goes through another series of cycles of being conquered, rising up in revolt, some autonomy, then being conquered. The Romans were the 3rd such invaders in 63 BC and remained in control there until 313 AD when Constantine conquered this land. However the people of Israel had been wiped out or scattered 300 years before Constantine arrived. In 73 AD, the last Israelite stronghold of 900 men, women and children fell to the Romans at Masada. And the Children of Israel were either dead or scattered all over the Middle East to escape with their lives. Only a tiny remnant of the poorest of the poor Jews were left in Jerusalem.

Now Satan was out to destroy the object of God's special love more than ever. He chased them down, kicking them out of their homes, raping, murdering, torturing them wherever they tried to hide, enticing them into anything that could distract them from loving God. Many times they repented, but it has been 2,000 years of running and assimilating into their new cultures enough to not stand out too much. And yet, most have kept the traditions of their forefathers in dedication to the outward signs of Judaism. However it is still the heart of His Beloved Israel that God is after.

It was in the middle of all this being conquered and revolting and being conquered that God enacted His plan. He sent own His son, Jesus as the promised Messiah, to become the way for the Jews to be reconciled to God after all, to do away with the daily sacrifices. Unfortunately for the Jews, they had a different picture in their minds for the way their Rescuer would look and behave. And most of them missed Jesus' coming.

So the torture by Satan and the decimation of God's Chosen People lasted about 2,000 years, but in the late 1800's God began to fulfill His promise to bring His people back to their Land. The original Land He gave promised Abraham! And on May 14, 1948, Israel was reborn. Who ever heard of such a thing?

Now, let's break it down and read the "why" bit in the Scripture:

In Leviticus 26:33, God made the original promise of what would happen if, after entering into this Covenant with Him, they broke their side of the agreement: The whole chapter relates the blessings and cursings of covenant. But 26:33 relates to the Land of Israel:

> Lev. 26:27-35: " 'If in spite of this you still do not listen to me but continue to be hostile toward me, then in my anger I will be hostile toward you, and I myself will punish you for your sins seven times over. You will eat the flesh of your sons and the flesh of your daughters. I will destroy your high places, cut down your incense altars and pile your dead bodies on the lifeless forms of your idols, and I will abhor you. I will turn your cities into ruins and lay waste your sanctuaries, and I will take no delight in the pleasing aroma of your offerings. **I will lay waste the land, so that your enemies who live there will be appalled. I will scatter you among the nations and will draw out my sword and pursue you. Your land will be laid waste, and your cities will lie in ruins.** Then the land will enjoy its Sabbath years all the time that it lies desolate and you are in the country of your enemies; then the land will rest and enjoy its Sabbaths. All the time that it lies desolate, the land will have the rest it did not have during the Sabbaths you lived in it.

In Deuteronomy's overview of the law it says the same thing: Deuteronomy 28:63-65 (NIV)

> Just as it pleased the LORD to make you prosper and increase in number, so it will please him to ruin and destroy you. You will be uprooted from the land you are entering to possess. Then the LORD will scatter you among all nations, from one end of the earth to the other. There you will worship other gods—gods of wood and stone, which neither you nor your fathers have known. Among those nations you will find no repose, no resting place for the sole of your foot. There

the LORD will give you an anxious mind, eyes weary with longing, and a despairing heart.

However God's heart has always been for the Jewish people like this:

Hosea 11:8-11 (New Living Translation)

> "Oh, how can I give you up, Israel?
>   How can I let you go?
> How can I destroy you like Admah
>   or demolish you like Zeboiim?
> My heart is torn within me,
>   and my compassion overflows.
> No, I will not unleash my fierce anger.
>   I will not completely destroy Israel,
>   for I am God and not a mere mortal.
>   I am the Holy One living among you,
>   and I will not come to destroy.
> For someday the people will follow me.
>   I, the LORD, will roar like a lion.
> **And when I roar,**
>   **my people will return trembling from the west.**
> **Like a flock of birds, they will come from Egypt.**
>   **Trembling like doves, they will return from Assyria.**
> **And I will bring them home again,"**
>   **says the LORD.**

Prophecy Fulfilled

The Lord said He would roar and they would come home. In the age in which we live He has roared, and they are coming! It began with a trickle even before the formation of the new nation of Israel. And by the 1980's and 90's it could have been called a flood. According to the Israeli Ministry of Foreign Affairs, between 1989 and 1996, 700,000 Jews immigrated to Israel from the former Soviet Union alone! But there are more out there. There were 2.5 million Jews on record there.[8] They came from war-torn European countries, and America, and Africa, and the surrounding Middle Eastern countries. Those are other great stories for another day!

Back to the Scriptures that spell out this destruction as prophecy before it happened: It makes me wonder how many times God tries to get our attention with warnings and signs before we get lambasted by the enemy.

Jeremiah 9:6-16

> You live in the midst of deception; in their deceit they refuse to acknowledge me," declares the LORD. Therefore this is what the LORD Almighty says: "See, I will refine and test them, for what else can I do because of the sin of my people? Their tongue is a deadly arrow; it speaks with deceit. With his mouth each speaks cordially to his neighbor, but in his heart he sets a trap for him. Should I not punish them for this?" declares the LORD. "Should I not avenge myself on such a nation as this?"
>
> I will weep and wail for the mountains and take up a lament concerning the desert pastures. They are desolate and untraveled, and the lowing of cattle is not heard. The birds of the air have fled and the animals are gone. I will make Jerusalem a heap of ruins, a haunt of jackals; and I will lay waste the towns of Judah so no one can live there.
>
> What man is wise enough to understand this? Who has been instructed by the LORD and can explain it? Why has the land been ruined and laid waste like a desert that no one can cross? The LORD said, "It is because they have forsaken my law, which I set before them; they have not obeyed me or followed my law. Instead, they have followed the stubbornness of their hearts; they have followed the Baals, as their fathers taught them." Therefore, this is what the LORD Almighty, the God of Israel, says: "See, I will make this people eat bitter food and drink poisoned water. I will scatter them among nations that neither they nor their fathers have known, and I will pursue them with the sword until I have destroyed them."

Because God is a faithful and because He entered into this Covenant with Abraham, He was obliged to allow His part of the curse to take place. Though many, MANY times, He had mercy, and put off judgment until the next generation. And yet He LOVED His people with an everlasting love. The baseline is not "crime and punishment." He is pursuing hearts that they would desire to please Him, not be "obligated" to perform the Law, and avoid sin. It is the same for us as Christians. He is after our hearts. His desire is that we love Him and minister to Him in worship, and that we steer clear of sin, not out of obligation, but out of our love for Him.

Jeremiah 31: 36-37

> Only if these decrees vanish from my sight," declares the LORD, "will the descendants of Israel ever cease to be a nation before me." This is what the LORD says: "Only if the heavens above can be measured and the foundations of the earth below be searched out will I reject all the descendants of Israel because of all they have done," declares the LORD.

And when the time of their punishment is fulfilled He promises to bring them back to Israel again: (selected verses from Jer. 31)

3 The LORD appeared to us in the past, saying: "I have loved you with an everlasting love; I have drawn you with loving-kindness. **4 I will build you up again and you will be rebuilt, O Virgin Israel**. Again you will take up your tambourines and go out to dance with the joyful.

8 See, I will bring them from the land of the north and gather them from the ends of the earth. Among them will be the blind and the lame, expectant mothers and women in labor; a great throng will return.

9 They will come with weeping; they will pray as I bring them back. I will lead them beside streams of water on a level path where they will not stumble, because I am Israel's father, and Ephraim is my firstborn son.

10 "Hear the word of the LORD, O nations; proclaim it in distant coastlands: 'He who scattered Israel will gather them and will watch over his flock like a shepherd.'

11 For the LORD will ransom Jacob and redeem them from the hand of those stronger than they. 17 So there is hope for your future," declares the LORD. Your children will return to their own land.

20 Is not Ephraim my dear son, the child in whom I delight? Though I often speak against him, I still remember him. Therefore my heart yearns for him; I have great compassion for him," declares the LORD.

23 This is what the LORD Almighty, the God of Israel, says: "**When I bring them back from captivity**, the people in the land of Judah and in its towns will once again use these words: 'The LORD bless you, O righteous dwelling, O sacred mountain.'

25 I will refresh the weary and satisfy the faint."

Ezekiel 20:40-42

> For on my holy mountain, the high mountain of Israel, declares the Sovereign LORD, there in the land the entire house of Israel will serve me, and there I will accept them. There I will require your offerings and your choice gifts, along with all your holy sacrifices. I will accept you as fragrant incense when I bring you out from the nations and gather you from the countries where you have been scattered, and I will show myself holy among you in the sight of the nations. **Then you will know that I am the LORD, when I bring you into the land of Israel, the land I had sworn with uplifted hand to give to your fathers.**

Wow is that amazing! God swore to bring them back, and He has fulfilled His word!

Ezekiel 28:25-26

> 'This is what the Sovereign LORD says: When I gather the people of Israel from the nations where they have been scattered, I will show myself holy among them in the sight of the nations. Then they will live in their own land, which I gave to my servant Jacob. They will live there in safety and will build houses and plant vineyards; they will live in safety when I inflict punishment on all their neighbors who maligned them. Then they will know that I am the LORD their God.'

Restoration of Israel (Isaiah 49:8-23)

8 This is what the LORD says: "In the time of my favor I will answer you, and in the day of salvation I will help you; I will keep you and will make you to be a covenant for the people, to restore the land and to reassign its desolate inheritances,

⁹ to say to the captives, 'Come out,' and to those in darkness, 'Be free!' "They will feed beside the roads and find pasture on every barren hill.

¹⁰ They will neither hunger nor thirst, nor will the desert heat or the sun beat upon them. He who has compassion on them will guide them and lead them beside springs of water.

¹¹ I will turn all my mountains into roads, and my highways will be raised up. ¹² See, they will come from afar—some from the north, some from the west, some from the region of Aswan."

¹³ Shout for joy, O heavens; rejoice, O earth; burst into song, O mountains! For the LORD comforts his people and will have compassion on his afflicted ones. ¹⁴ But Zion said, "The LORD has forsaken me, the Lord has forgotten me."

¹⁵ **"Can a mother forget the baby at her breast and have no compassion on the child she has borne? Though she may forget, I will not forget you!** ¹⁶ **See, I have engraved you on the palms of my hands**; your walls are ever before me. ¹⁷ Your sons hasten back, and those who laid you waste depart from you. ¹⁸ Lift up your eyes and look around; all your sons gather and come to you. As surely as I live," declares the LORD, "you will wear them all as ornaments; you will put them on, like a bride.

¹⁹ "Though you were ruined and made desolate and your land laid waste, now you will be too small for your people, and those who devoured you will be far away.

²⁰ The children born during your bereavement will yet say in your hearing, 'This place is too small for us; give us more space to live in.' ²¹ Then you will say in your heart, 'Who bore me these? I was bereaved and barren; I was exiled and rejected. Who brought these up? I was left all alone, but these—where have they come from?'"

²² This is what the Sovereign LORD says: "See, I will beckon to the Gentiles, I will lift up my banner to the peoples; they will bring your sons in their arms and carry your daughters on their shoulders.

²³ Kings will be your foster fathers, and their queens your nursing mothers. They will bow down before you with their faces to the ground; they will lick the dust at your feet. **Then you will know that I am the LORD; those who hope in me will not be disappointed.**"

Combating Replacement Theology

In case anyone wonders whether "the Christian Church" has replaced Israel in God's promises, take a look at verses 15 & 16. "…I will not forget you. See I have engraved you on the palm of my hand…" This modern idea that God gave up on the Jews when they rejected or killed Jesus is called "replacement theology," and it is just plain wrong. A lie. It is prevalent in many mainline churches throughout the world. My question to those who believe this idea is this: If God chose to change His mind on His promise to love and care for His original people, how can Christians believe that He will not change His mind on accepting them through the blood of Jesus Christ? If God is not a "promise-keeping God" throughout all the ages, then Christianity is a sham.

Thank God that is not the case! God keeps all of His promises and we can trust Him.

Endnote: Famous Jews throughout the Ages

Jews have won more Nobel prizes than seems possible. They make up ¼ of 1% of the world population and have been granted 22% of the Nobel prizes for contributions of excellence to humankind. Notably, 9% of the Peace Prizes, 19% of chemistry awards, 26% of physics awards, 28% of medicine awards, and a whopping 41% of all economics awards have been won by Jewish men and women! Is it a conspiracy or a trick? No, it is the divine favor of God that is without end resting on the people He chose.

Some famous people you may not have realized are part of God's chosen people: Einstein, Sigmund Freud, Galileo, Christopher Columbus, Isaac Singer (sewing machine), Levi Strauss (jeans!), Joseph Pulitizer, Steven Spielberg, Groucho Marx, composers Mendelssohn, George Gershwin, William Schuman, modern songwriters Carol King, and Carly and Paul Simon, and Oscar Hammerstein II (of Rogers & Hammerstein).

Oh yeah, and Mary and Jesus!

CHAPTER 2
LESSON: THE FORMATION OF AN ISRAELITE NATION

Teacher Notes: It is helpful to read straight through Genesis before this lesson.

Topics: A nation through Abram, His call, the promise at Bet El, Genesis 15 Covenant, name change, Isaac/Ishmael problem, Jacob.

Timeline for Abraham
Okay, quick time line placement of Abraham: Adam, then 1,656 years pass until the Great Flood. The tower of Babel which was during Peleg's lifetime between 1,757 and 1,996 years after creation (1 Chronicles 1:19 & Genesis 10:25) would have occurred just 100 to 200 years after flood waters receded, depending on WHEN in Peleg's lifetime Babel's disbursement occurred. And then just 190 years later Abram (and brothers Nahor & Haran) is born. Meaning that Peleg could have been alive when Abram was born!

Abram was born to his father Terah, an idolmaker in Ur (of the Chaldees). Of course, according to Paul Johnson's *History of the Jews*, that would have been before the Chaldees actually lived there, but it is a reference point which has been archeologically proven. It is currently called Dhi Qar, Iraq.

The Call
The scripture reads as if Terah may have been given the first call to leave Ur (Gen 11:31). One of Abram's two brothers (Haran) had already died in Ur (Gen 11:28) leaving a son, Lot, behind. The extended family packed and left Ur. They traveled about 600 miles to a town called Haran (sound familiar? Abram's brother has the same name!! but according the notes in the NIV study Bible, it is spelled differently in the Hebrew language and therefore not named after him.)[9] In the city of Haran the same moon god that was primarily worshipped in Ur was also worshipped there, so Terah may have felt very comfortable staying there. Terah didn't seem to have the will to leave that place called by his son's name, which was a thriving caravan town by the 19th century BC and was ruled by Ammorites in the 18th century BC.[8] So, the family waited/lived there a number of years. Terah died at age 205, and they buried him in

Haran, and Abram and Sarai took their nephew Lot and all their possessions and continued on the adventure God had invited them on. Abram was 75 years old when they left Haran (Gen 12:4). Makes me wonder how many earlier generations or people might have had the same invitation from God, yet only Abram's choice to follow an unknown (yet One, True) God qualified him for the promise that God made to him about becoming a great nation.

Here is the promise of Gen 12: 2-3

> I will make you into a great nation and I will bless you;
> I will make your name great, and you will be a
> blessing. I will bless those who bless you, and whoever
> curses you I will curse; and all peoples on earth will be
> blessed through you.

A pretty big deal, especially since Abraham had no heir at age 75 for this nation to come from! So, they arrived (Gen 12:5) in the land of Canaan, and Abram traveled the land as far as Shechem. The Lord appeared again to Abram there and gave him some more specifics. "To your offspring I will give this land" (Gen 12:7). As Abram continued his wandering journey southward, he built an altar at Bethel (*Beit El*) and worshipped God there. Then they continued toward the Negev (desert wilderness in terrain) and ran into a famine. So they continued even farther south, going into Egypt. Abram began a bad pattern of behavior with the Egyptians at this early point in Jewish history.

Apparently, Sarai was very beautiful, and Abram was worried that he would be killed so Pharaoh could take her as his wife. So Abram told Sarai to lie and reveal only that they were brother/sister. They actually were half brother/sister (Gen 20:12, same father), but they neglected to mention to the Egyptians who inquired that they were also married!

And things happened just as Abram feared. Sarai was taken into Pharaoh's palace as his wife, but Abram was treated well because they had told everyone she was only his sister. Sarai must have been one very hot lady to be worth killing over at a minimum age of 65, after several years of wandering in varied climates with no Oil of Olay! However, God made sure Pharaoh found out. (Gen 12:17-20)

> But the LORD inflicted serious diseases on Pharaoh and his household because of Abram's wife Sarai. So Pharaoh summoned Abram. "What have you done to me?" he said. "Why didn't you tell me she was your wife? Why did you say, 'She is my sister,' so that I took her to be my wife? Now then, here is your wife. Take her and go!" Then Pharaoh gave orders about Abram to his men, and they sent him on his way, with his wife and everything he had.

Now keep in mind before judging Abram in this situation: this is nearly 500 years BEFORE the 10 Commandments have been given. There is not yet any law governing the soon-to-be patriarchs of the Jewish faith, even though the major tenets of integrity have become engrained into our society today.

Abram, Sarai and Lot went north back to the Promised Land, wandering from place to place until finally returning to the spot where Abram had originally worshipped God (*Beit El*) and been promised the land.

During all this wandering Lot and Abram had both become rich with servants and livestock and there was not enough land resources to support both of them living together any more. So they went up a mountain in Beit El and Abram told Lot, "Choose the land that you want to live on and raise your family and your livestock. I will take whatever land you do not want." Lot chose all the best parts, most fertile land and cities of the Jordan Valley for himself. And Abram took the leftovers.

The Jordan River Valley is today still some of the most fertile land in Israel. It is where much of their food is grown for feeding all of Israel, and even for export! Millions of the flowers imported to Europe come from the Jordan River Valley.

Before Abram moved on south toward the Negev desert, God renewed the promise of the Land again (Gen 13:14-18).

> The LORD said to Abram after Lot had parted from him, "Lift up your eyes from where you are and look

north and south, east and west. All the land that you see I will give to you and your offspring forever. I will make your offspring like the dust of the earth, so that if anyone could count the dust, then your offspring could be counted. Go, walk through the length and breadth of the land, for I am giving it to you." So Abram moved his tents and went to live near the great trees of Mamre at Hebron, where he built an altar to the LORD.

Genesis 14 sets up a strange little historical tidbit that shows how important a place in Abram's life his family was. Several kings surrounding Abram allied together and went to war. They ended up carting off Nephew Lot and his household as POWs from Sodom. (Before Sodom was incinerated). Abram put together an army of 318 of his "trained men born in his household" and they walloped them, chasing them as far north as Damascus! (a *long* way! Approximately 4-5 hours by car).

It is after this little incident of retrieving Lot that Abram connects with the king of Salem, Melchizadek. Salem is Jerusalem and the king of Salem is the first prophetic picture we see of Jesus. Melchizadek is both a king and a priest of the Most High God. And the concept of tithing is introduced in this event recorded in Gen 14:18-20.

Then Melchizedek king of Salem brought out bread and wine. He was priest of God Most High, and he blessed Abram, saying, "Blessed be Abram by God Most High, Creator of heaven and earth. And blessed be God Most High, who delivered your enemies into your hand." Then Abram gave him a tenth of everything.

Abram demonstrates the depth of his growing relationship with the Almighty God when Melchizadek offers Abram the goods that they had brought back from their conquest. Abram will accept nothing for himself, only his men's share, because he doesn't want anyone to have an opportunity to claim that Abram's success came from their help. He wants all success to be credited to God's blessing over his life. THAT is commendable!

Perhaps it is this attitude and state of character that somehow qualified Abram for what was to come next:

The COVENANT of Gen 15

The Lord visited Abram in a dream and confirmed His promise of an heir again. (Gen 15 selected verses, bold mine).

[4]Then the word of the LORD came to him: "This man (Eliezer) will not be your heir, but a son coming from your own body will be your heir." [5]He took him outside and said, "Look up at the heavens and count the stars—if indeed you can count them." Then he said to him, "So shall your offspring be." Abram believed the LORD, and He credited it to him as righteousness.

[7]He also said to him, "I am the LORD, who brought you out of Ur of the Chaldeans to **give you this land to take possession of it.**"

[13] Then the LORD said to him, "Know for certain that **your descendants** will be strangers in a country not their own, **and they will be enslaved and mistreated four hundred years. [14]But I will punish the nation they serve as slaves, and afterward they will come out with great possessions.** [15]You, however, will go to your fathers in peace and be buried at a good old age. [16]In the fourth generation your descendants will come back here, for the sin of the Amorites has not yet reached its full measure."

[17]When the sun had set and darkness had fallen, a smoking firepot with a blazing torch appeared and passed between the pieces. [18]On that day the LORD made a covenant with Abram and said, "**To your descendants I give this land, from the river of Egypt to the great river, the Euphrates- [19]the land of the Kenites, Kenizzites, Kadmonites, [20]Hittites, Perizzites, Rephaites, [21]Amorites, Canaanites, Girgashites and Jebusites.**"

This is the first mapping out of the land that God was promising to Abram and his descendants forever. It is a lot of land and bigger than even the current boundaries of modern Israel. In this promise statement is also the foretelling of the first exile in Egypt and how long it will last, 400 years from the 4th generation (Joseph and the 11 brothers).

Ishmael/Isaac Issue

Beautiful, beautiful promises of the Lord. But Abram was like us: in a hurry to *help* God fulfill His word. Enter Sarai's suggestion of conceiving their promised son (& nation) through their servant Hagar. The three of them go ahead with this plan, and when it works, things become so unbearable between Sarai and Hagar that the pregnant Hagar runs away. Here is what happens next in Gen 16: 9-16.

> Then the angel of the LORD told her, "Go back to your mistress and submit to her." The angel added, "I will so increase your descendants that they will be too numerous to count."
>
> The angel of the LORD also said to her: "You are now with child and you will have a son. You shall name him Ishmael, for the LORD has heard of your misery. He will be a wild donkey of a man; his hand will be against everyone and everyone's hand against him, and he will live in hostility toward all his brothers." She gave this name to the LORD who spoke to her: "You are the God who sees me," for she said, "I have now seen the One who sees me."... So Hagar bore Abram a son, and Abram gave the name Ishmael to the son she had borne. Abram was eighty-six years old when Hagar bore him Ishmael.

A prophetic word about this son as well, but to his mother, (not Abram)! In case you don't know, I will spoil the surprise: Ishmael became the father of the Arab nations. We will catch up with Ishmael and his progeny in lesson 9.

I can imagine that Abram must have thought that this son, Ishmael, was the son God promised all along. It had been about 11 years since the original promise of a son. And life went along normally for 13 more years. I assume Abram invested in Ishmael as the son of promise for all those years. Until one day God had a surprise for his friend Abram. Genesis 17 is another central event to the formation of the nation of Israel. God confirms the covenant of Gen 15 again, with more details. Abram (meaning: exalted father) is 99 years old now, Sarai is 89. God changes their names to Abraham (Father of many) and Sarah. Then God drops this bomb: "Oh yeah, Ishmael is NOT the son I promised you. His name will be Isaac, and he will be born to the two of you in the next year" (Gen 17:19 paraphrased). It has now been 25 years since the original promise, and still it is not fulfilled. No wonder Abraham's faith was counted as righteousness!

I find it interesting that God named the boy Isaac meaning "laughter" before Sarah was informed that she would conceive and laughed. (Gen 18:10-15).

This encounter with the Lord also brought with it something that Abraham had to do to show he was buying into this covenant with the Lord and His promises. Circumcision. And Abraham's whole household of males was circumcised that same day! THAT is whole-hearted commitment! And from here on out, Abraham's descendants would be circumcised on the 8th day of life.

In current Jewish culture, the Circumcision Ceremony is called a *Brit Melah* or Brit for short, and it is done in the synagogue by a *mohel* or the family's rabbi. It's usually followed by a small party or celebration with close friends and family. It is an honor to be invited to a Brit.

Back in our timeline, the whole Sodom and Gomorrah debacle occurs, complete with Lot's wife turning into a pillar of salt. Then Abraham again does the whole "Sarah is my sister" bit, with Abimelech, king of Gerar. (Gen 20). It is after Sarah is returned to her husband that she conceives Isaac and then gives birth to him (Gen 21). What a year of changes and transition they had to endure that year. Abraham was 100, and Sarah was 90.

A short while later, when Isaac was weaned (age 2 to 7), Sarah asked Abraham to force Hagar and Ishmael to leave their household. Abraham did not want to, but the Lord told him to do as Sarah asked (Gen 21:12), and so they were sent away. But the Lord had promised to also make Ishmael into a great nation because he was Abraham's seed. And the Lord took care of them in the Wilderness of Paran. Ishmael married a woman from Egypt (Gen 21:21)

Another important event occurs now. The sacrifice of Isaac. The rest of the patriarchs (Isaac, and his coming son, Jacob) won't be studied in such detail, but Abraham was a prototype, and so many things occurred in his life that speak prophetically of the nation of Jews.

God spoke to Abraham as recorded in Genesis 22, "Then God said, 'Take your son, your only son, Isaac, whom you love, and go to the region of Moriah. Sacrifice him there as a burnt offering on one of the mountains I will tell you about.'"

We will set aside the questions about the morality of murder, the need for obedience, the desire for faith, the question of whether God would raise Isaac from the dead, and focus only on this: the sacrifice was to take place on Mount Moriah. Moriah will become a prominent feature as the home of all the future temples. But it is where God provided the FIRST lamb to die in place of Isaac. It happened countless times over the generations leading up to Jesus, with perfect lambs offered each year at Passover celebrations and offered as sin offerings at the temples built on this same Mount Moriah. Jesus was the LAST lamb needed. He gave up His life, lived without blemish, to pay for our sin *in the same location*. (Complete Isaac story can be found in Genesis 22).

Abraham is willing to give up his promised son in obedience to the Lord's voice.

> "I swear by myself, declares the LORD, that because you have done this and have not withheld your son, your only son, I will surely bless you and make your descendants as numerous as the stars in the sky and as the sand on the seashore. Your descendants will take possession of the cities of their enemies, and through

your offspring all nations on earth will be blessed, because you have obeyed me" (Gen 22:16-18).

Now, 3700 years later, it is just as God said. Even after the countless times that the Jewish people have been under annihilation edicts, God's word stands true forever. In the early 1940's there were nine million Jews who would stand up and be counted alive at this one point in history. Remarkable! And a fulfillment of this promise. Of course after Hitler, there were only 3 million left.

Time for a little fast forward. Isaac married Rebekah (Rivkah in Hebrew) who was the granddaughter of Abraham's brother Nahor. Isaac and Rebekah had twins, Esau and Jacob (Yacov in Hebrew). Wow! Lots of sibling rivalry there. (Stories found in Genesis 25 through 36.) The most important information of this time is that God changes Jacob's name to "Israel" after an encounter with Him in Beit El when Jacob buys into the promise that God gave his grandfather, Abraham, of making of him a great nation. (Notice that it is the same location as the land choosing with Lot and Abram) (Gen 28:10-22). Wonder what would have happened if Jacob had said, "No thanks, I'll keep my old name."

Interestingly, Isaac and Ishmael together buried their father, Abraham, who died at age 175 in the cave of Machpelah near Mamre. (Gen 25:9)

Jacob had 12 sons (by 4 women—which I'm sure kept him on his toes) the second youngest of whom was named Joseph. Through an unfortunate series of sinful events of brotherly hatred, betrayal, and nearly murder, Joseph was sold to passing slave traders, Midianites (a people group who will come into play again with Moses), and Joseph was transported to Egypt. (Gen 37:12-36). In Egypt, Joseph was sold to Potipher, an officer of Pharaoh, and captain of his guard.

At this time Jacob's (Israel's) family was just his sons and their children who were little more than wandering shepherds. Hardly even able to be called a tribe.

Joseph excelled greatly for Potipher and took care of everything in his household. However, when Joseph rebuffed his master's wife's come-ons, she kicked up a ruckus in her humiliation and Joseph, though he escaped with his life, ended up in prison. Let me just say, prison in Egypt, where there was not a great deal of sanctity of life, was miserable! However, Joseph ends up on the top of the pile again. He is running the prison by Gen 39:21-23.

> But while Joseph was there in the prison, the LORD was with him; he showed him kindness and granted him favor in the eyes of the prison warden. So the warden put Joseph in charge of all those held in the prison, and he was made responsible for all that was done there. The warden paid no attention to anything under Joseph's care, because the LORD was with Joseph and gave him success in whatever he did.

Through some more "random" events like dream interpretations, Joseph ends up going from prison to second in command of the whole land of Egypt, under only Pharaoh himself! Talk about a crazy turn of events that only God could orchestrate! Because of Joseph, and his planning before a famine, the whole Middle Eastern world was saved from starvation.

Joseph's brothers came to Egypt (not knowing he was their brother, of course) to beg to buy bread. Through several long trips back and forth from Canaan to Egypt, the 12 brothers were reconciled and invited, along with their whole families, to move to the Land of Goshen in Egypt, to feed their flocks there.

And so All Israel (numbering about 70) lived in Egypt, and moved there without a fuss. But Joseph and his generation died. (Exodus 1)

> Now Joseph and all his brothers and all that generation died, but the Israelites were fruitful and multiplied greatly and became exceedingly numerous, so that the land was filled with them.
>
> Then a new king, who did not know about Joseph, came to power in Egypt. "Look," he said to his people, "The Israelites have become much too numerous for us. Come, we must deal shrewdly with them or they will become even more numerous and, if war breaks

out, will join our enemies, fight against us and leave the country."

So they put slave masters over them to oppress them with forced labor, and they built Pithom and Rameses as store cities for Pharaoh. But the more they were oppressed, the more they multiplied and spread; so the Egyptians came to dread the Israelites and worked them ruthlessly. They made their lives bitter with hard labor in brick and mortar and with all kinds of work in the fields; in all their hard labor the Egyptians used them ruthlessly. (Ex 1:6-14)

Oh boy, oh boy, oh boy (*oy vey!*)! did that ever backfire! However, God knew what He was doing. He had foretold this very thing to Abraham. It would last 400 years, and then...

Next lesson we will pick up with how God redeemed a rag-tag couple of million slaves into a nation!

40

CHAPTER 3
LESSON: THE FIRST EXILE

Teacher notes: it is helpful to Read Exodus chapters 2, 3, 6-12, 14-15 before class

Topics covered: Egypt. 400 years to Moses. Prophecy from Abraham and fulfillment.

Egypt

As far as I can tell there is no literature recording exactly how the Hebrews became enslaved to the Egyptians. But history follows pattern, and it probably started as discrimination leading to a series of major events which each escalated in ferocity against the Hebrews.

As an aside, since the name "Jews" is derived from the name Judah—the 4th son of Israel/Jacob. It is highly unlikely that the Hebrews would have been called "Jews" until they returned from the second exile (~515 BC) and they were mostly survivors of the Tribe of Judah.[10]

Exodus 1-3 records the early life of Moses, who in Israel's history has become the current most-revered character. *Moshe*, is how he is called in Hebrew. He was born into an enslaved Hebrew household in the Tribe of Levi, with an older sister and brother, Miriam and Aaron, during a time of much panic among the Hebrews. The Pharaoh was afraid of an uprising (and losing his free labor) so he ordered the midwives to kill all the baby boys. When they did not, "Then Pharaoh gave this order to all his people: 'Every boy that is born you must throw into the Nile, but let every girl live'" (Ex 1:22).

Moses

So into this society, Moses was born. His mother managed to keep him hidden for three months, and in a very amazing turn of events that you can read in Exodus 2, Jocobed entrusted her son Moses to the Lord's care, and he ended up being raised by the daughter of Pharaoh as her own son, a prince of Egypt. She was the one who named him Moses, because she "drew him from the water" (which is what Moses means).

Apparently, Moses knew enough about his own history to identify with the Hebrews as his own people: "One day, after Moses had grown up, he went out to where his own people were and watched them at their hard labor" (Exodus 2:11). After Moses killed one of the Egyptian slave drivers who was beating a Hebrew slave, he ran away to the desert, and after 40 years the Lord appeared to him in a bush that was on fire, but not burning up and He said,

> "I have indeed seen the misery of my people in Egypt. I have heard them crying out because of their slave drivers, and I am concerned about their suffering. So I have come down to rescue them from the hand of the Egyptians and to bring them up out of that land into a good and spacious land, a land flowing with milk and honey" (Ex 3:7).

According to Bernard Reich in his book *A Brief History of Israel* (2005), the nation of Israel was probably delivered from the rule of Ramses II, around 1266 BC.[10]

It was a complex series of meetings with Moses approaching Pharaoh, requesting their freedom, doing signs and wonders, being denied, then being told, "ok," then the Pharaoh changing his mind. Ten times this goes on before the Hebrews are finally sent away carrying the riches of Egypt as foretold to Abraham, 400 years earlier. Incidentally, RIGHT on schedule.

The Exodus & First Passover
This freedom event has become central in Israeli and Biblical history, and it is celebrated by Jewish families every year at Passover. An interesting way that God demonstrated His higher power to both His people and the Egyptians is that each of the plagues God afflicted on the Egyptians was associated with one of the 10 main gods the Egyptians worshipped.

1. Water of Nile River turned to blood—Hapi—Egyptian god of the Nile
2. Frogs from the Nile River—Heket—Egyptian god of fertility, water & renewal, had the head of a frog.
3. Lice from the dust of the earth—Heb—Egyptian god of the dust of the earth
4. Swarms of flies—Khepri—Egyptian god of creation, movement of the Sun, rebirth. Had the head of a fly.

5. Death of cattle/livestock—Hathor—Egyptian goddess of love & protection, usually depicted with the head of a cow.
6. Ashes turned to boils and sores (thought to be smallpox)—Isis—Egyptian god of medicine & peace.
7. Hail rained in the form of fire—Hut— Egyptian goddess of the sky
8. Locusts from the sky—Seth— Egyptian god of storms & disorder
9. Three days of complete darkness—Ra— Egyptian god of the sun
10. Death of the firstborn—Pharaoh—the god of ultimate power in Egypt

Correlation with pictures can be reviewed at hubpages.com.[11]

A couple of misconceptions I have heard over the years about the parting of the Red Sea (or the Sea of Reeds) can pretty much be traced to Hollywood movies or folklore.

1. *The Ten Commandments* movie shows about 25,000 extras who had been cast to walk across the dried Red Sea seabed as the water stood up on either side of them. The deliverance was also depicted like this in the animated version of the same story, Disney's *Prince of Egypt*. In all likelihood, it was closer to several million Hebrews, plus all their belongings and livestock, who had to cross the sea overnight. In order for a crossing this massive to happen, the gap God created and dried out for them would have had to be MILES wide! Picture that!

2. The second misconception that tried to explain away the miracle is that the Red Sea was just in "low season" and had nearly dried up anyway. Hmmm, seems like an even bigger miracle with that explanation, since the entire Egyptian army drowned as they tried to pursue the Israelites across it. Hmm.

In the 1970's Ron Wyatt found and retrieved chariot wheels from the seabed of Red Sea (Gulf of Aqaba)[12] They were of the particular design used during the 18th dynasty of Ancient Egypt.

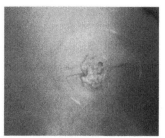

Chariot wheel fixed to axels standing
at attention on the seabed. See
www.wyattmuseum.com

A 4-spoked chariot wheel
on the Red Sea seabed.
Found in 1998. See
www.wyattmuseum.com

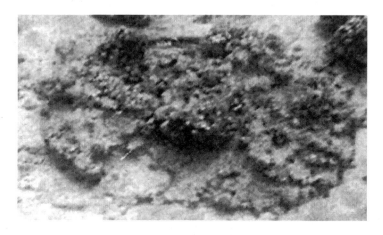

Chariot wheel found encrusted in coral by Ron Wyatt in the Red Sea.
Photos used by permission from www.wyattmuseum.com.

Once the Egyptian army pursuers were dead, the newly-free people of
Israel had their first official worship service as a free nation. (Ex 15: 19-
21)

> When Pharaoh's horses, chariots and horsemen went
> into the sea, the LORD brought the waters of the sea
> back over them, but the Israelites walked through the
> sea on dry ground. Then Miriam the prophetess,
> Aaron's sister, took a tambourine in her hand, and all
> the women followed her, with tambourines and
> dancing. Miriam sang to them:

"Sing to the LORD, for he is highly exalted.
The horse and its rider he has hurled into the sea."

According to Johnson in his book, *A History of the Jews,* "We sometimes lose sight of the sheer physical fact of the successful revolt and escape of a slave-people, the only one recorded in antiquity...this unique demonstration of God's mightiness on their behalf was the most remarkable event in the whole history of nations."[13]

Three days-without-water later, however, they were grumbling and complaining to Moses. But God provided all they needed: Water turned from bitter to sweet, manna (bread) rained down from heaven, water gushed from a rock, the Amalekites were destroyed in battle, and personal problems that arose from living in community were resolved by a new system of judges (courtesy of Jethro, Moses's Midianite father-in-law). Three months into this journey of becoming (timeline from Ex 19:1), they had no given law to abide by, except to only gather the manna needed per person, per day, and gather a double portion on Friday, so they could rest on the Sabbath.

> This unique demonstration of God's mightiness on their behalf was the most remarkable event in the whole history of nations

Mount Sinai
Then enter the Moses on Mount Sinai event. Moses is invited into God's presence on Mount Sinai and the Law is handed down from God. Exodus 20-31 records the laws, beginning with the Ten Commandments that God put in place for Israel. Laws concerning the worship at the altar, servants, violence, animal control, responsibility for property, morality, justice, the Sabbath, three annual Feasts of the Lord (Passover, Harvest/Sukkot/Tabernacles & First Fruits), offerings, the ark of the covenant, and the tabernacle.
Exodus 23:20-33 records what the Lord promises to do for Israel if they will obey His Law:
"See, I am sending an angel ahead of you to guard you along the way and to bring you to the place I have prepared. Pay attention to him and listen to what he says. Do not rebel against him; he will not forgive your rebellion, since my Name is in him. If you listen carefully to what he says and do all that I say, I will be an enemy

to your enemies and will oppose those who oppose you. My angel will go ahead of you and bring you into the land of the Amorites, Hittites, Perizzites, Canaanites, Hivites and Jebusites, and I will wipe them out. Do not bow down before their gods or worship them or follow their practices. You must demolish them and break their sacred stones to pieces. Worship the LORD your God, and his blessing will be on your food and water. I will take away sickness from among you, and none will miscarry or be barren in your land. I will give you a full life span.

"I will send my terror ahead of you and throw into confusion every nation you encounter. I will make all your enemies turn their backs and run. I will send the hornet ahead of you to drive the Hivites, Canaanites and Hittites out of your way. But I will not drive them out in a single year, because the land would become desolate and the wild animals too numerous for you. Little by little I will drive them out before you, until you have increased enough to take possession of the land.

"I will establish your borders from the Red Sea to the Sea of the Philistines, and from the desert to the River. I will hand over to you the people who live in the land and you will drive them out before you. Do not make a covenant with them or with their gods. Do not let them live in your land, or they will cause you to sin against me, because the worship of their gods will certainly be a snare to you."

And Israel agrees to the covenant, but when Moses is called back up on Mount Sinai, and stays longer than the people are expecting, they turn their backs on their new covenant with God by convincing Aaron to build them a golden calf to worship (Ex 24:1-8).

Then the LORD said to Moses, "Go down, because your people, whom you brought up out of Egypt, have become corrupt. They have been quick to turn away from what I commanded them and have made themselves an idol cast in the shape of a calf. They have bowed down to it and sacrificed to it and have said, 'These are your gods, O Israel, who brought you up out of Egypt.'

What a spit in the face of God who had just delivered them from bondage. Big long explanations on why a calf and not some other animal can be found,[14] but it comes down to that the calf was representative of the pagan rituals that they knew. They wanted to go back to what they knew, to hold onto what they could see, instead of embracing the leadership of a God that they could not see.

The Children of Israel did repent when Moses came down Mount Sinai, and the covenant was renewed (Ex 34), but we will leave this story for now as the entire company of Israel wanders in the desert for the next 40 years (though not as a punishment for this idolatry, it was something else that we will get to soon).

Eventually, the giving of the Law became a celebrated event called *Simchat Torah*. A holiday celebrated at the end of Sukkot each year. Today the Jewish people dance with the Torah scrolls with much exuberance! This takes place in the synagogues around the world and in a joyous celebration in front of the Western Wall in Jerusalem.

Traditionally, it is during the time that Moses had on the mountain with God while Moses was hidden in the cleft of the rock and God passed by exposing the backside of His glory to Moses (Ex 33:21-23) that Moses received the account of the beginning of the world that is recorded in Scripture, both the Jewish Torah and the Christian Old Testament. If all that knowledge was revealed just by glimpsing the backside of His glory, how much more will we understand when we behold Him from the front?!

CHAPTER 4
LESSON: THE DESERT AND CONQUERING THE PROMISED LAND

Topics: the desert, Joshua, conquering the Promised Land, question of a loving God, the Philistine problem, Gath and current Gaza problem, Judges, Give us a king, divided kingdom, chart of the Kings of Israel & Judah.

The Desert

Picking up where we left off, with Israel agreeing to the Covenant with God after the golden calf incident, when they were given the Law. They built the Ark of the Covenant, and the mobile Tabernacle to house the Ark in according to the instructions and specifications given by God. They set up camp wherever the cloud by day or fire by night stopped (Numbers 9:15-23).

It is hard to pin down exactly how long the Israelites had been wandering in the desert to this point because the dates from different scholars are slippery, perhaps 6 months to 2 years, but about 1312 BC[15] 12 men were chosen, one from each tribe, to spy out the land God had given Abraham 400 years earlier. For 40 days, the spies wandered and observed while Israel camped on the east side of the River Jordan. Then the spies brought back some whompin'-sized fruit from the Land into the camp and declared that it flowed with milk and honey (Numb 13:27).

Deut 1:19-37 is an overview account that Moses gives of this event just before he dies.

The spies all agreed that the Land was great, but then Joshua and Caleb's report differs from the other 10 spies. The 10 declare, "the people who dwell in the land are strong; and the cities are fortified and very large; moreover we saw the descendants of Anak there (giants)," But Caleb quieted the people before Moses and said "Let us go up at once and take possession, for we are well able to overcome it."

The people of Israel had a choice at this point: who to believe. Then the 10 came back with a stronger whine (Numb 13:31-33)

> "We can't attack those people; they are stronger than we are." And they spread among the Israelites a bad

48

report about the land they had explored. They said, "The land we explored devours those living in it. All the people we saw there are of great size. We saw the Nephilim there (the descendants of Anak come from the Nephilim). We seemed like grasshoppers in our own eyes, and we looked the same to them."

And unfortunately Israel believed the bad report and cried all night with fear (Numb 14:1). The people complained and threatened to choose a new leader to take them back to Egypt! (What were they planning to say? "Sorry, we didn't mean jump up and leave you in the lurch like that. Could we be your slaves again? pretty please?") They were about to stone Moses when the glory of Lord came into the camp! (Numb 14:10).

God was ready to wipe them out fully and start over with Moses. But Moses, ever the leader, interceded with God for Israel. He boldly reminds God that God said He was longsuffering, abundant in mercy, forgiving iniquity and transgression. And so God relents and says:

I have forgiven them, as you asked. Nevertheless, as surely as I live and as surely as the glory of the LORD fills the whole earth, not one of the men who saw my glory and the miraculous signs I performed in Egypt and in the desert but who disobeyed me and tested me ten times-not one of them will ever see the land I promised on oath to their forefathers. No one who has treated me with contempt will ever see it. But because my servant Caleb has a different spirit and follows me wholeheartedly, I will bring him into the land he went to, and his descendants will inherit it.

And it was for their disbelief that the Israelites were turned around and sent to wander in the desert for 40 years, (one year for each day the spies were spying) until all the people age 20 and older had died, except Joshua and Caleb. Then God pronounced a capital punishment sentence over the 10 spies who brought back the bad report: they died on the spot by a plague before the Lord (Numb 14:37).

Israel made one futile attempt to conquer the Land on their own, by reasoning that the Lord had forgiven them when the spies had been destroyed. But neither the Ark of the Lord's presence nor Moses went with them. The Amalakites drove them back as far as Hormah (Numb 14:39-45).

Then the Hebrews wandered and wandered and wandered. During the wandering Moses became a friend of God, yet he sinned against God once himself, by striking a rock in anger instead of speaking to it to provide water for the people he was leading. Moses' punishment was that he would not be the one to lead the Children of Israel into the Promised Land. (pretty stiff punishment, but the principle that God holds leaders to a higher standard is established here). And so, at age 120, Moses died on Mt Nebo, and Joshua son of Nun, became Israel's new leader.

All Israel mourned Moses for 30 days on the plains of Moab (across the Jordan River from Jericho).

Joshua and the Conquering of the Promised Land

God ordered Joshua to begin taking possession of the land little by little over the years, so that the people of Israel could settle the cities as they captured them. They started with a spectacular win in Jericho. Followed by a devastating and embarrassing loss at Ai, because someone stole spoils of war that they were ordered not to take. After Achan (the thief) was killed and his whole family and possessions stoned, burned, and buried by rocks, the people were more diligent about following orders. Ai was attacked again, and taken.

City after city was taken; king by king fell.

How can a loving God kill people?
One problem that a lot of people have with this total conquering is the killing of the women and children, even babies. It makes me squirm myself! However, these cultures were accepting of some pretty rotten practices, idolatry and sins. They worshipped Satan (aka Ba'al or Molech) and while there is certainly room for forgiveness of sins and restoration and healing through Jesus Christ now, He had not come yet. And Satan had laid claim to those people of Canaan through the generations of sins that had been committed such as ritual murder, temple prostitution, and homosexuality, and they called it all worship!

Tendencies toward certain sinful practices are passed down soul to soul, generationally. Children can be born with spiritual strongholds and according to Exodus 20:5, the sins of the parents are visited down to the 3rd and 4th generations. Obviously, we have a choice whether to sin or not.; God gave us each a conscience. We know right from wrong. But apparently, God had had it with these Canaanite nations. Their sin and sin patterns had to be destroyed in order for the Nation of Israel, Beloved in covenant with God, to stand a chance of surviving to become the holy people, set apart, that God called them to be.

"But it is not fair," you might argue. The Canaanites didn't have the Bible to tell them they were sinning. I have to then ask, has it made a difference for you? Has having the written Word of God kept you from all sins? Obviously, no, "for all have sinned and come short of the Glory of God."

And secondly, these written laws of God were in effect before they were written down. Their consequences were in effect since the beginning. For example: Did the law of gravity exist and function before it was written down? And if you are not aware of the law of gravity, does that mean it does not apply to you and you are not held accountable to it?

Taking this analogy further, I ask myself, why should I be angry with a God who, though He knows the law of gravity is functioning, decides to expose the trumping principles of lift (flight) to someone? He is certainly not obligated to tell everyone everything. Does it mean He is not the loving God He claims to be because He chooses to expose His higher law to the People called by His name? I think not.

I am sure this could lead to some very rigorous small group or dinner table conversations. Enjoy!

Back to the story:
When God first told Moses that He was going to take them into the land of the Canaanites, He referenced (Ex 3:8) six cultures living there: Canaanites, Hittites, Amorites, Perizzites, Hivites, and Jebusites. Where did these folks come from? All of these clan-cultures except the Perizzites trace their ancestry to Noah's son Ham, through Ham's son

Canaan (Gen 10:15-18). In both Gen 10:7 and in Gen 10, the Perizzite clan is treated as a separate people group. Numb 13:29 and Joshua 11:3 both refer to them living in the hill country. So something made them different and separate, but from Scripture, it is not clear. Anyway, Joshua and the Israelites launched a major campaign against them all, city by city. Sometimes the kings would form alliances with one another, but the Lord, through Joshua, still struck them down. Joshua 11:16-23 gives a summary of this:

> So Joshua took this entire land: the hill country, all the Negev, the whole region of Goshen, the western foothills, the Arabah and the mountains of Israel with their foothills, from Mount Halak, which rises toward Seir, to Baal Gad in the Valley of Lebanon below Mount Hermon. He captured all their kings and struck them down, putting them to death. Joshua waged war against all these kings for a long time. Except for the Hivites living in Gibeon, not one city made a treaty of peace with the Israelites, who took them all in battle. For it was the LORD himself who hardened their hearts to wage war against Israel, so that he might destroy them totally, exterminating them without mercy, as the LORD had commanded Moses.
>
> At that time Joshua went and destroyed the Anakites from the hill country: from Hebron, Debir and Anab, from all the hill country of Judah, and from all the hill country of Israel. Joshua totally destroyed them and their towns. No Anakites were left in Israelite territory; only in Gaza, Gath and Ashdod did any survive. So Joshua took the entire land, just as the LORD had directed Moses, and he gave it as an inheritance to Israel according to their tribal divisions. Then the land had rest from war.

But there were still people groups occupying the Land that the Lord was giving the Children of Israel, namely the Philistines of Gath, who became a constant thorn in Israel's side, even today [though the current occupants of Gath (aka Gaza) are not Philistines]. According to Joshua 13:1-6, there was still much land to conquer, especially the north, the

Golan region, and along the coast in the current cities of Gaza, Ashkelon, Ashdod.

> When Joshua was old and well advanced in years, the LORD said to him, "You are very old, and there are still very large areas of land to be taken over.

> "This is the land that remains: all the regions of the Philistines and Geshurites: from the Shihor River on the east of Egypt to the territory of Ekron on the north, all of it counted as Canaanite (the territory of the five Philistine rulers in Gaza, Ashdod, Ashkelon, Gath and Ekron—that of the Avvites from the south, all the land of the Canaanites, from Arah of the Sidonians as far as Aphek, the region of the Amorites, the area of the Gebalites ; and all Lebanon to the east, from Baal Gad below Mount Hermon to Lebo Hamath.

> "As for all the inhabitants of the mountain regions from Lebanon to Misrephoth Maim, that is, all the Sidonians, I myself will drive them out before the Israelites. Be sure to allocate this land to Israel for an inheritance, as I have instructed you.

The Philistine Problem:

Over the years, some part of Israel was usually at war with these people groups that they failed to conquer right off the bat with Joshua before he died. Clan leaders came and went, priests, judges, prophets came and went, but there was no one leader over them all except God.

There was much corruption and lawlessness, and also much good that went on in Israel during these first years as a nation. Deborah, Gideon, Sampson and Ruth are some of the individuals that stood out during these 200 years. Then Samuel was born ~1070 BC[16] to Hannah and Elkanah, and Samuel seems to be a pivotal point in Israel's existence.

Samuel grew up from his boyhood with the priest Eli in the service of the Tabernacle in Shiloh, where the center of worship in Israel had been for about 400 years. He listened and obeyed God to the same level that Moses and Joshua had. I Samuel 3:19 says, "The LORD was with

Samuel as he grew up, and he let none of his words fall to the ground. And all Israel from Dan to Beersheba recognized that Samuel was attested as a prophet of the LORD."

Israel seemed to be doing well under Samuel's leadership, but they began clamoring for a king, like all the other nations. Samuel warned them that they would not function well under a king because the Lord God should be their leader, but they asked again and again. So, God told Samuel to anoint Saul, from the tribe of Benjamin, to be king over Israel. And he did.

As king, Saul united the tribes into a single army which fought pretty well when they had been commanded by the Lord to fight an enemy and failed utterly when they had not.

The Philistines were a constant threat. After two years as king, Saul attacked a garrison of Philistines (in actuality it was Saul's son Jonathan who did it, as told in 1 Sam 13) with 3,000 men. It really just stirred up a hornet's nest, because the Philistines then gathered 30,000 chariots PLUS 6,000 horsemen and "people as the sand which is on the seashore in multitude" at Michmash against the Israelites. (1Sam 13:5). Israel had a "freak out moment" and hid themselves in caves, thickets, and holes in the ground in the area of Gilgal. Hosea 9:15 records that the Lord says that He began to hate Israel at Gilgal.

> Because of all their wickedness in Gilgal,
> I hated them there.
> Because of their sinful deeds,
> I will drive them out of my house.
> I will no longer love them;
> all their leaders are rebellious.

I had always wondered what happened there for God to say such a thing. The following events may be why:

King Saul waited seven days for Samuel to come so he could offer the sacrifice and peace offerings before battle as prescribed by the Lord. Samuel had told him that he would be there in seven days, but Saul had not seen him yet, so he took matters into his own hands. Saul ordered that the burnt offerings and peace offerings be brought to him and he made them himself.

And then Samuel showed up.

"What have you done!?" Samuel asked. Then Saul began his excuses. (My, how humanity is consistent throughout the generations. Thirty-five hundred years later, don't we do the same thing?) Saul's punishment or perhaps better terminology is "lack of blessing" is this:

> "You acted foolishly," Samuel said. "You have not kept the command the LORD your God gave you; if you had, he would have established your kingdom over Israel for all time. But now your kingdom will not endure; the LORD has sought out a man after his own heart and appointed him leader of his people, because you have not kept the LORD's command" (1 Sam 13:13-14).

The Lord diffused the situation with the Philistines through Jonathan. And they all lived to fight another day (and fight again they did!). Saul continued his warring with the peoples on every side, and "there was fierce war with the Philistines all the days of Saul" (1 Sam 14:52). Though Saul reigned in Israel for 42 years, his downfall began early in his career. The breaking point was when the Israelite Army was fighting against the Amalakites (1 Sam 15). God told Saul though Samuel the Prophet to "utterly destroy all that they have, and do not spare them. But kill both man and woman, infant and nursing child, ox and sheep, camel and donkey" (1 Sam 15:3). However, Saul spared King Agag and the best of the sheep and other animals.

And the Lord said, "I greatly regret that I have set up Saul as king, for he has turned back from following me, and has not performed my commandments," and Samuel cried out to the Lord all night.

Even though Saul made excuses and then even apologized, it was not enough. "For to obey is better than sacrifice" (1 Sam 15: 22). Obedient hearts are what God is looking for. And so for his disobedience, Saul was rejected as king.

It is not often in life that we as Christians get to know what we did or did not do which disqualifies us from parts of our destiny. Which little inner prompting did we choose not to follow through on? And the inverse is also true: We are not often privy to the anointings and levels of authority that we qualify ourselves for through being obedient in all things, no matter how small and seemingly insignificant! Let's obey with right hearts.

Samuel the Prophet then accomplished what Saul had not, by hacking Agag into pieces. And Samuel never went to see Saul again. Therefore, King Saul never heard the Word of the Lord again for the rest of his life!

Shortly thereafter, David, son of Jesse, a boyish shepherd of the fields was anointed king of Israel by Samuel the Prophet. However, it would be years and years before he ascended to the actual role and function of king. But, David was in training all that time for his calling to be Israel's king. David, from a young man, lived his life in the way that God was looking for Israel, his Beloved, to live.

David ended up worshiping on his harp to calm King Saul's nerves when the "distressing spirits troubled him" (1 Sam 16:14-23). When the Philistines rose up again, sending out the giant Goliath of Gath to taunt the Israelites, cursing them and challenging the power and authority of their God, David took him on. David was not out for fame nor the prize offered by King Saul, but he was defending the honor of the Lord's name. David prophesied to Goliath what he was going to do: take his head from him and feed the camp of the Philistines to the birds and beasts so that "all the earth shall know that there is a God in Israel" (1 Sam 17:46).

And David did all that he prophesied!

While David is the "golden king" of Israel from the perspective of Christianity, he is only mildly revered from the modern Jewish perspective. For Christians King David presents as the worshiping king who was "after God's own heart." He embodied humility and patience as he waited for God's timing to ascend the throne, not killing or even allowing his men to kill God's anointed king. One who even with all his warring and killing, praised God thoroughly. He brought the Ark of the

Covenant to a home he created for it in Jerusalem. He danced with all his might to the absolute humiliation of his wife, Michal. (Michal became barren for all her days because of this judgment she made against her husband's exuberant worship). David created a place in every day life for worship of Jehovah. He bestowed honor back to the priesthood for the Levites. He set musicians and worshipers in place, so that worship rose 24/7. He constantly cried out to the Lord for help.

Yes, there was the awful incident with Bathsheba. Adultery and murder, the death of their child. The prophet Nathan brought conviction, and David bowed in genuine repentance. And there was restoration.

David's family skills left a lot to be desired. His sons vied for his throne. Jealousy and treason abounded in his offspring. One son (Amnon) raped David's daughter (Tamar), and another son (Absalom) killed Amnon for it. David exiled the avenger. (II Samuel 13). But Solomon, David's second child with Bathsheba, became his successor as the third king of Israel.

David's place in the history of the kings of Israel is seen by Modern Jews as great and having three major significances. "First he conflated the regal...in a way that was never possible for Saul. Samuel had no immediate successor and much of his spiritual authority devolved on David. David, despite his occasional wickedness, was evidently a man of deep religious feeling."[17] David took a kingship that had previously been about warring to gain the Promised Land and independence and transformed it into "a glittering institution which combined religious sanction, oriental luxury and new standards of culture...the popular masses found it exciting and satisfying."[17] The second significance in Jewish culture is that "David's position as king-priest seemed to have received divine blessing since his purely military achievements were unrivalled."[17] The third and perhaps most long-lasting is that "David established a national and religious capital which was also his own conquest,"[18] in Jerusalem, The City of David.

Solomon started out well as the third king of Israel. When God offered him anything he wanted, Solomon asked for wisdom to rule the people. God was very pleased with the request and gave him wisdom such as has never been known before or since. God also gave Solomon great riches (I

Kings 3). In the 480th year after the Beloved Israel escaped Egypt, and in the 4th year of his reign, Solomon began to build the glorious Temple of Yahweh in Jerusalem (I Kings 6). It was situated on top of Mount Moriah (II Chron. 3:1). Does this mountain's name sound familiar? Remember, it is the same location Abraham took Isaac to sacrifice him and the Lord provided a ram in his place!

Over the years, Solomon's dedication waned. Probably because of all the foreign wives he took in alliances with other nations. God had specifically warned Israel about marrying outside their faith. The women brought their gods with them, and life in Israel started a downhill slide.

Divided Kingdom
When Solomon died, there was not a consensus among the people of Israel as to who the rightful heir to the throne was. Jeroboam, Solomon's mighty man and chief officer, was anointed king by the prophet Ahijah the Shilonite over the ten tribes of the north. (Shilonite just means "from Shiloh" which by the way is a nice little town these days, and whose mayor gave me and some friends a hiking tour of the place in 2007!)

The people of the southern part of the kingdom, Judah, (made up of the tribes of Judah and Benjamin) received Rehoboam (Solomon's son) as their king. However, he was an evil, power- and money-hungry man who imposed even more taxes on the people than his father had.

Israel and Judah entered into years of kings who were generally each more evil than the last. Idol worship became an accepted-as-normal practice in Israel. Ashtoreth poles for worship went up on every high place. Firstborn children were sacrificed both by water and fire to Molech. Beloved Israel became a stench to God's nostrils. However, every once in a great while a good man would ascend the throne and begin to turn Israel back to the Lord, such as Jehoshaphat, Hezekiah and Josiah. However, never was every high place brought down into submission to Yahweh, nor the Temple and Israel cleansed for worship at the same time. It would take several generations of good kings in a row to restore Israel fully. Unfortunately, the godly kings never seemed to have enough time to invest both in their sons (successors) and the cleansing of Israel. The following is a listing of the kings of Israel and Judah.[19, 20, 21]

The Divided Kingdoms

Dates (BC)	Israel (Northern)		Judah (Southern)	Dates (BC)
			Rehoboam	922-915
922-901	Jeroboam I		Abijah	915-913
901-900	Nadab		Asa	913-873
900-877	Baasha			
877-876	Elah			
876	Zimri	Tibni	Jehoshaphat	873-849
876-869	Omri			
869-850	Ahab			
850-849	Ahaziah		Jehoram	849-843
849-843	Joram (Jehoram)		Ahaziah	843
843-815	Jehu		Athaliah (non-Davidic Queen)	843-837
815-802	Jehoahaz		Joash	837-800
802-786	Jehoash (Joash)		Amaziah	800-783
786-746	Jeroboam II		Uzziah (Azariah)	783-742
746-745	Zachariah		Jotham	750-742

745	Shallum		Jotham (king)	742-735
745-737	Menahem			
737-736	Pekahiah			
736-732	Pekah		Ahaz	735-715
732-724	Hoshea			
721	Fall of Samaria			
			Hezekiah	715-687
			Manasseh	687-642
			Amon	642-640
			Josiah	640-609
			Jehoahaz	609
			Jehoikim (Eliakim)	609-598
			Jehoiachin (Jeconiah)	598-597
			Zedekiah (Mattaniah)	597-587
			Fall of Jerusalem	587

60

According to I Kings 11:33-34, here is why the kingdom was divided:

> I will do this because they have forsaken me and
> worshiped Ashtoreth the goddess of the Sidonians,
> Chemosh the god of the Moabites, and Molech the god
> of the Ammonites, and have not walked in my ways,
> nor done what is right in my eyes, nor kept my
> statutes and laws as David, Solomon's father, did.
>
> But I will not take the whole kingdom out of Solomon's
> hand; I have made him ruler all the days of his life for
> the sake of David my servant, whom I chose and who
> observed my commands and statutes.

So from the time of Solomon's death until 1948, the Land of Israel had not been whole!

CHAPTER 5
LESSON: THE SECOND EXILE

Topics: because of evil in the Land, ancient sieges, 10 lost tribes, Assyria and Babylon take over the Land, Jeremiah, Esther & Daniel, The Macabees, Destruction of Solomon's Temple on 9th of Av.

Over the two year period of 722 to 720 BC the Assyrians came into Israel (the northern 10 tribes) and carted off many of the Israelites into slavery and distributed them across their other land holdings. "The Assyrian conquerors invented a new policy towards the conquered: in order to prevent nationalist revolts by the conquered people, the Assyrians would force the people they conquered to migrate in large numbers to other areas of the empire."[22]

As far as take-overs go, it was mild for these northern tribes. Though I suppose our modern definition of "mild" differs greatly from those people's definition who were uprooted from their homes and lives. There would have had to have been some force and fear behind this great migration. The Biblical version is found in II Kings 17. The Israelites had been paying tribute (i.e. holding at bay) the Assyrian king, Shalmaneser, for a number of years and then stopped paying. Shalmaneser discovered that Israel's king, Hoshea, had sent envoys to Egypt, which apparently Shalmaneser thought was outside the scope of their arrangement. So the Assyrian king took King Hoshea and imprisoned him and began laying siege to Israel. This siege lasted for 3 years. Then "the king of Assyria captured Samaria and deported the Israelites to Assyria. He settled them in Halah, in Gozan on the Habor River, and in the towns of the Medes" (II Kings 17:6).

God allowed His Beloved people to be conquered because of their great disobedience. He desired relationship with them, and they had a pattern of turning back to Him when they finally got miserable enough without Him. God was not "being mean" or unreasonable. Israel had agreed to the terms of the covenant. If they worshiped other gods, they were breaking the covenant that offered God's protection from these invading nations.

It was not as if they were dabbling with drunkenness and missing a Shabbat service every once in a while either. The stink of sin rising up to the heavens included worshipping stones and stars; they set up incense and Ashurah poles on every high place (there are a LOT of high places on the mountains of Israel!); they worshipped Baal, practiced sorcery and witchcraft; and they sacrificed their sons and daughters to these idols by fire. Usually the infants were burned alive. God had warned Israel through the prophets Hosea, Amos, Micah, and Zephaniah specifically to repent, and Israel refused. II Kings 17:9 says that they did evil things in secret. They would not have tried to hide if they did not know it was sin.

Therefore God removed Israel from His presence (II Kings 17:18).

An Ancient Siege
As "mild" as the Assyrian take over was, a siege in ancient days was not pleasant for those trapped inside the walls of cities, surrounded by their enemies with no access to fresh supplies of food or water or troop reinforcements. An army generally surrounded the city and sat in wait for surrender or negotiations to begin, but they would push the timeline forward with scare tactics and small attacks, and bombardments or mining under the walls to weaken the city's defenses. The Assyrians designed siege towers that could also be used as battering rams. They were much more sturdy than the previously used ladders to scale the walls, and they could launch flaming arrows or diseased dead animals inside the besieged city from the top of the tower.[27] After any animals inside the siege zone had been consumed for food, the people inside would eventually get so desperate as to eat each other, and when they finally surrendered they would be more subdued and manageable because of weakness, and probably shame, thus marching them off to resettle in unknown lands would have been "mild" for the conquering army versus compelling a strong, rebellious and angry mob to leave their homes.

The Ten Lost Tribes
Israel was marched off and disappeared into the Assyrian Empire, not to be heard from again as a whole, even to this day. They are known as the 10 Lost Tribes. There are researchers and archeologists who specialize in searching for them or any trace of what became of them. There are pockets of remnants of Israel that have been found in India, Nigeria,

Ghana, and all over Africa and in Afghan regions, China, even the UK. Because of a similarity of customs and traditions, there is speculation that the Japanese people and Native Americans could also be related to the 10 Lost Tribes. There are currently DNA and blood tests that can prove or disprove a person's Jewish ancestry. It is a fascinating subject worthy of an in-depth study because of God's Word which says that ALL 12 tribes will once again be returned to the Land of Israel (Rev 7:4). However we will not be able to concentrate on this topic nor delve into the current "Ephraimite Movement."

About 135 years after the northern tribes disappeared, the southern tribes of Judah had not changed their ways of idolatry and sin either, besides a small window of repentance under King Hezekiah while the Assyrians were busy up north carting away their cousins. The Assyrians had been all set to conquer Judah too, but King Hezekiah paid them off with all of the gold used to build and decorate the Temple. However, the people of Judah believed that God would save them even though the Assyrian soldiers mocked and taunted them. And God did save them.

But once again Judah, like her sister Israel, fell into sin. The Babylonians arrived in 586 BC and destroyed the region, Jerusalem and the Temple. They carted off the Jews into exile, and all but a small remnant of the poorest Jews became captives in the Babylonian Empire. It was King Nebuchadnezzar who ruled Babylon during Judah's destruction.

> The Babylonian conquest brought an end to the First Jewish Commonwealth (First Temple period) but did not sever the Jewish people's connection to the Land of Israel. The exile to Babylonia, which followed the destruction of the First Temple (586 BC), marked the beginning of the Jewish Diaspora. There, Judaism began to develop a religious framework and way of life outside the Land, ultimately ensuring the people's national survival and spiritual identity and imbuing it with sufficient vitality to safeguard its future as a nation.[23]

The Lord's glorious Temple that King David designed and his son Solomon built was destroyed on the 9th of Av. (Remember this date. It is one of infamy, and now one of national fasting in Israel because of the evil that befalls the Jews throughout history on this date.)

Jeremiah's "70 years" Prophecy is fulfilled and seen by Daniel
Jeremiah was one of the prophets who unveiled what would happen to Judah if she did not repent. He prophesied that they would be captive for 70 years (Jer. 25:11-12) and that Babylon (even though they were incited by God to capture Israel) would be held responsible for their treatment of the Jews. Jeremiah was captured in Jerusalem in 586 BC when the Babylonians came, and he was given a choice to go to Babylon or to stay in Jerusalem. He stayed and witnessed the utter destruction of the holy city and the Babylonian Army carting off all the temple treasures (Jer. 38-40). When the Jews were settled into their new area, the smartest young men were rounded up, made eunuchs, renamed and trained for the king's purposes in literature, histories, maths, sciences, and for advising in wisdom. Shadrach, Meshach and Abed-Nego (remember their fiery furnace story?), along with Daniel, were some of these young men (Dan. 1:3-9). Ezekiel was prophesying from the Exile in Babylon. They were also somewhat contemporaries of Esther, though certainly not of the same generation. Esther was made Queen to Ahasuerus (or Xerxes I) in Persia around 480-ish BC (after Darius conquered Babylon and had already started to let Jews go back to their homeland if they wanted to. Many decided to stay in Persia in the new lives they had made for themselves over three to four generations of living there.).

A few Jews flourished in exile as is seen in Daniel's elevation of influence of at least 4 kings that he mentions (historical evidence suggests that there were a couple more after Nebuchadnezzar that Daniel does not reference). But most Jews did not, as you can gather from Esther's story. The enemy of God stirred hate in the hearts of their captors and their neighbors toward God's chosen people. During this unsettling time the Bible records the stories of the *Handwriting on the Wall* at Belshazzar's feast on the eve of Darius's conquering of Babylon and of *Daniel in the Lion's Den* under King Darius the Mede.

When Daniel saw that the 70 years was almost completed, he began praying and repenting on behalf of his exiled nation. Daniel also prospered under King Cyrus the Persian, when he conquered Babylon. King Cyrus, under direction of the Holy Spirit, made this decree in the 70th year of Judah's exile:

'The LORD, the God of heaven, has given me all the kingdoms of the earth and he has appointed me to build a temple for him at Jerusalem in Judah. Anyone of his people among you—may his God be with him, and let him go up to Jerusalem in Judah and build the temple of the LORD, the God of Israel, the God who is in Jerusalem. And the people of any place where survivors may now be living are to provide him with silver and gold, with goods and livestock, and with freewill offerings for the temple of God in Jerusalem' (Ezra 1:2-4).

Ezra and Nehemiah lead the first and second *Aliyah*

So God had not only turned the heart of a pagan king toward Himself to fulfill His promise of 70 years in exile, God had the king **pay** for the return and the rebuilding of the Temple which had been laid to ruin! (insert gleeful shout!) Doesn't that kind of sound like when the Hebrews left Egypt with the riches of that nation? About 50,000 Jews made the trek back to Israel in the first wave led by Ezra (Ezra 2:64-65), and they are listed by head of family. (These Jews who returned and settled in the northern area of Israel later became known as Samaritans.) Haggai and Zechariah were contemporaries of Daniel in prophecy, though they were prophesying from Jerusalem, not from exile (Ezra 5:1). But when Ezra returned, he found that those left behind had forgotten to keep the Laws of the Lord, they had intermarried with non-Hebrew women, and had done nothing to restore the temple.

Ezra's first order of business after the four-month journey home was to celebrate the Feast of Tabernacles. They began to offer the daily sacrifices and the new moon sacrifices (Ezra 3:4-5) and to clean out the ruined Temple. As with any work project in Jerusalem, there was resistance by the locals. They sent complaints and tattlings to King Artaxerxes. The work was halted by force until King Darius found their permission in the archives and reinstated the work. (Ezra 5-6).

Nehemiah was a prophet of God who had a day job of being King Artaxerxes's cup bearer (can we say ancient sommelier?) After appearing sad before the king one day because of his people's plight, Nehemiah was sent to Judah to rebuild the city. He took with him labor and tribute and permissions to use the king's timber (Neh. 2: 4-9). When Nehemiah returned home to Jerusalem, he began to rebuild the ruined ancient walls. Because of harassment, the families who were rebuilding their sections of the wall, kept one man on guard with a spear for every man working on the stones from daybreak until sunset (Neh. 4:21-22). Then they and their servants stood guard at night. It took 52 days to rebuild the walls.

Nehemiah ended up functioning in the role of governor of Israel. And the people divided up to live in their cities and some in Jerusalem, but when the seventh month came, they made their way back to Jerusalem to celebrate the Feast of Tabernacles (again). Ezra who was the priest at the time, read the Book of the Law of Moses (Torah) to the people in the open square (Neh. 8:1-2). And the people worshipped and bowed with their faces to the ground and said "Amen." They feasted and became still to celebrate the holy day. On the 24th day of the month, they gathered in a solemn assembly again, in sackcloth with fasting, they separated themselves from the foreigners among them, and Israel confessed her sin for a quarter of a day and worshipped before the Lord for the next quarter of the day (Neh. 9:1-3). As recorded in Nehemiah 10, Israel reaffirmed the Covenant with the Lord and placed their seals on it.

How excited and pleased must the Lord have been! He had brought them back to the Land at the appointed time and they turned their hearts to Him.

The Maccabees and Hanukkah
After the Jews were up and running again under governors for about 400 years, unfortunately, they returned to their cycles of corruption and repentance, return to sin and reform, worship and rejection of God. So deep was this scar of a sin nature upon their hearts, that as a people, even those called by God's own name, they could not remain faithful to the covenant. They could not love God by following rules. Even so, God loved them in every generation!

They had been conquered by Alexander the Great as he swept his way across the known globe. (Which I suppose they would not have called a "globe" since there was still another 1,800 years to come of assuming the world was flat.) Alexander introduced the religion of Hellenism and the language of Greek every where he went.

> In every location which he (Alexander) conquered, he
> would order his troops to marry the local women so
> that a race of Greeks might soon be born. He also
> commanded that the Greek language be taught to all
> conquered peoples, and that Greek was to be the
> official language of the empire.[24]

Alexander died in 323 BC at a whopping age of 33, with no heir (oh, the irony). His conquest was divided into four parts to be run by his generals. This division was prophesied in Daniel 8:21-22 as Gabriel interprets a vision given to Daniel during Belshazzar's third year of reigning.

> The shaggy goat is the king of Greece, and the large
> horn between his eyes is the first king. The four horns
> that replaced the one that was broken off represent
> four kingdoms that will emerge from his nation but will
> not have the same power.

The Land of Israel was given to Ptolemy Lagi, and the Greek wars in Israel began as Alexander's four generals continued to fight amongst themselves to gain control over more territories. Seleucus was ousted from ruling Babylon by Antigonus, so he went to help Lagi rule his territory.

> After the *Battle of Ipsus* (301 BC), Seleucus
> succeeded in taking all the territory previously held by
> Antigonus; the kingdom of Lysimachus was also
> absorbed into the Seleucid Dynasty. Thus, with the
> exception of the small Macedonian kingdom, the entire
> empire was now controlled by the Seleucids in the
> North and the Ptolemies in the South. Caught right in
> the middle of these two struggling factions was
> Palestine, and it became the source and site of
> constant conflict between the Seleucids and the
> Ptolemies. For the first 100 years or so the Ptolemies
> held the upper hand in the struggle over Palestine, the
> home of the people of Israel…. For the most part, they
> were very good to their Jewish subjects, although they
> did tax them quite heavily.[24]

There were many Ptolemies who ruled, and then the family was defeated by Antiochus III. The Jews were initially happy that the 200 years of fighting would finally be over. But Antiochus turned out to be worse than the Ptolemies. You see, Hannibal (yes, the Hannibal of the fighting elephants) had just been defeated by the Romans and he sought refuge with Antiochus. Hannibal convinced Antiochus to invade Greece somehow, then

> Rome promptly declared war on Antiochus. The Romans defeated Antiochus in 190 BC, and made him pay dearly for his alliance with Hannibal. He was forced to pay enormous amounts of money, and to surrender his navy and his war elephants. To insure that Antiochus continued making his payments, the Romans took his youngest son to Rome where they kept him hostage for twelve years. This young boy was later to return to the Seleucid Empire and assume the throne under the name *Antiochus Epiphanes.*" [24]

In the meantime, the high priest's office in Jerusalem was for sale to the highest bidder. Jason and Melenaus were the two men who paid to be installed into the office. This outraged the Jews who were holding true to the Law. Some of them became outspoken about this abuse; they were known as the Hassidim, meaning the "pious ones." According to Maxey's research,[24] the modern Hassidic Jews trace their roots back to these men and women.

In 168 BC, Antiochus went to war against Egypt, but was stopped by Popilius Laenus, a Roman, who ordered him to get out and never return. So Antiochus took out his humiliation and fury on Jerusalem, slaughtering the people and destroying the city walls. Antiochus had the Jewish Scriptures destroyed and

> he and his soldiers brought prostitutes into the Temple and there had sex with them in order to defile the Temple. He also issued orders that everyone was to worship the Greek gods, and he established the death penalty for anyone who practiced circumcision, or who observed the Sabbath or any of the Jewish religious feasts and sacrifices.
>
> The cruelty of Antiochus in enforcing these new laws against the Jews became legendary. An aged scribe by the name of Eleazar was flogged to death because he refused to eat the flesh of a swine. In another incident, a mother and her seven young children were each

butchered, in the presence of the Governor, for refusing to worship an idol. In yet another incident, two mothers, who had circumcised their newborn sons, were driven through the city and then thrown to their deaths from the top of a large building.

The final outrage for the pious Jews of the land came when Antiochus sacked the Temple and erected an altar there to the pagan god Zeus. Then, on December 25, 168 BC, Antiochus offered a pig to Zeus on the altar of God. This was the last straw! The Jews had taken all they were going to take from these oppressors. The stage was set for a large-scale rebellion of the Jews against the Seleucids. This famous rebellion is known in history as the *Maccabean Revolt*.[24]

There was an old priest of the Lord, Mattathias, who had five sons who all lived a little way north of Jerusalem in a village called Modein (which is still there today). They were sometimes called the Maccabees, meaning "the hammers", though their actual ancestry is via the Hasmoneans.[24] The whole family was zealous for the Lord and His honor. When the temple and altar of the Lord was defiled and some officers were sent into the villages to force the priests to make sacrifices to the pagan gods, Mattathias was the priest they would have forced to do this vile thing.

A Jewish man in the village stepped forward to volunteer to make the sacrifice so that his priest would not have to defile himself. Which on the surface sounds kind and self-sacrificing, however it was a sin motivated out of fear. Fear of what the officers and soldiers would do if the people did not fall into line worshipping these false gods they had brought into God's own Land. Mattathias killed the Jewish man and the king's soldiers. Then he destroyed the pagan altar and stirred up the people by running through Modein shouting, 'Let everyone who is zealous for the Law and who stands by the covenant follow me!' (I Maccabees 2:27). "He and his sons, along with a good number of followers, fled to the mountains of the Judean wilderness."[24] In the Judean Mountains, the Maccabees began to launch a guerrilla war against Antiochus.

When Mattathias died, his son Judah took the lead. He had one of the best military minds ever known. Judah continually beat back the generals who came against him at great odds, such as 50,000 army troops against 6,000 poorly equipped rebels. When Antiochus realized he had trouble on his hands, he gathered 60,000 troops and 5,000 cavalry and went after Judah. Judah managed to muster 10,000 men and they prayed to Yahweh for deliverance. God came through, as He always does when His people humble themselves, pray and believe, and the Jews won a huge victory over this gigantic army.

Judah then decided to liberate Jerusalem, and to cleanse the temple.

> The Maccabees reclaimed the Holy Temple in Jerusalem. They cleaned the Temple, removing the Greek symbols and statues. When Judah and his followers finished cleaning the temple, they rededicated it. On the 25th day of the month of Kislev in 164 BC, the Temple was purified and rededicated.[25]

It was three years to the day after the pig was offered to Zeus on God's altar, that the temple was rededicated to God with much celebration and worship.

When the Maccabees arrived in Jerusalem though, they found that the oil used to burn in the lamps always before the Lord had been defiled. There was only enough unspoiled oil to burn for one day! The oil had to be manufactured according to God's specifications by the priests with a certain recipe given in the Torah. But they lit the menorah anyway, in order to begin to honor God the way He should be worshipped, and they began the process of getting the oil and ingredients they would need. It took a week to gather and make the holy oil.

And in a miracle such as had not been seen in centuries, the one-day supply of undefiled oil lasted for EIGHT days! The celebration of this miracle continues today as the Jewish people celebrate Hanukkah, the Festival of Lights, by lighting 8-branch menorahs called Hannukiahs (ha-na-KEY-uh) every night for 8 nights.

In 163 BC, the new Greco-Syrian king Lysias, tried to take over Jerusalem again. This time he was prepared and sent an army of 120,000 men and 32 war elephants who met Judah and his Macabbees. Judah was not able to crush the enemy, and retreated to Jerusalem after killing only 600 of Lysias' men. Lysias planned to starve those holed up in Jerusalem through a siege, but he received word that his own throne and capital city was at risk. So he offered Judah peace and religious control in exchange for political support for the Seleucid Empire. Judah and the Jews agreed.

The remaining sons of Mattathais also ruled. Jonathan first and then Simon. But the times were plagued with civil wars and uprisings and power seizes and murders. In between the unsettling times, the Jews were peaceful and prosperous though. When Mattathaia's son Simon was murdered in 135 BC, the Maccabean Revolt came to a swift end.[29]

There were power struggles every few years between 135 BC and 63 BC when the steamroller of the Roman Empire pressed into the Middle Eastern world. Two religious sects of Judaism had been warring with each other for control of the Land for years, so Pompey swept in to put an end to it and killed 12,000 Jews in Jerusalem and again the Temple of the Lord was defiled when Pompey entered the Holy of Holies!

But based on your knowledge of dates, I am sure you are already anticipating what will happen next!

CHAPTER 6
LESSON: THE 3ᴿᴰ EXILE AND THE 3 HERODS

Topics: Roman Invasion, Herod and successors, Jesus on the scene, What were the Jews looking for? Messianic prophecies chart, Messiah vs. Christ, Roman Occupiers

We left off with Pompey sweeping up a Jewish rebellion. A couple years later a man named Antipater was rewarded for squashing yet ANOTHER civil war in the Land of Israel with leadership of "Judea," as the Holy Land was currently being called.

Pompey was having some trouble by this time with a man who was rising in influence and power, named Julius Caesar. At a battle in 48 BC, Pompey was killed and Julius Caesar became the supreme ruler of the Roman Empire. Antipater managed to convey his switched loyalty to Caesar and remained in place as the ruler of Judea

> Julius Caesar also manifested a very lenient attitude toward the Jewish people throughout his kingdom, and granted them many special favors, among which was the right of full religious free
> dom. A year after Julius Caesar came to power Antipater died, and his son *Herod* became Procurator of Judea. Three years later, in March, 44 BC, Julius Caesar was assassinated.[26]

As you might remember from a high school Shakespeare course, there was a power struggle among three men after Julius Caesar was murdered. A man named Octavian came out on top, taking the reigns of leadership of the Roman Empire, and he took the name *Augustus*. He ruled until 14 AD. If Augustus sounds familiar to you, it might be from the scripture passage oft quoted at Christmas from Luke 2.

> In those days Caesar Augustus issued a decree that a census should be taken of the entire Roman world. (This was the first census that took place while Quirinius was governor of Syria.) And everyone went to his own town to register.

Antipater's son Herod ruled Judea beginning in 37 BC and became known as "Herod the Great." He built his leadership experience by functioning as the governor of Galilee during his father's reign. He is an odd, yet central, figure in Jewish history in that "Herod was both a Jew and an anti-Jew; an upholder and benefactor of Graeco-Roman civilization, and an oriental barbarian capable of unspeakable cruelties."[27] Herod was a builder of massive projects and sought to make his name remembered like Solomon's greatness. He built cities, palaces, the great harbor of Caesarea, and libraries and citadels in Judea, and in an early form of philanthropy, Herod sent money abroad to the Jews of the Diaspora (2nd Exile) to build beautiful synagogues, libraries, baths, and charities. "His life was dedicated to getting and spending on a gigantic scale."[27] But juxtaposed to this charity was his ease of executing anyone he felt threatened by, especially if there was a family relationship. Herod killed or had killed: his nephew, wife, brother-in-law, mother-in-law, and two sons! "He behaved with paranoid suspicion and reckless brutality."[27]

In relation to the Jewish religion though, Herod was a man of "separation of church and state." The first order of business when he assumed power in Jerusalem was to execute 46 Sanhedrin leaders who tried to uphold the Law of the Torah. He did not try to snatch the role of high priest as some previous leaders had done; he did not try to sell it either. Herod turned the office of High Priest into an official post, which, of course, he assigned. Most often he invited the more progressive Jews from outside Judea, from the Diaspora in Egypt or Babylon, to fill the post. The Jews outside Jerusalem were more likely to be open to Greek-style thinking or Hellenistic religious views mixed with their Judaism. I imagine that the men Herod brought in were less likely to have a following of people who would rise up against Herod's power, thus his imported High Priests were more controllable.

The palaces Herod the Great built for himself included Antonia, Herodium, Cypros, Machaerus, and Masada. Masada was a fortress cut out of the stone mountains of the Judean wilderness, designed and stocked to be used as a place of escape if Herod was ever attacked. "As a matter of fact if they hadn't closed the list of the wonders of the ancient world before his time, Herod would probably have added three more to list. Almost all archeologists and students of architecture of the ancient world appreciate that he was one of the greatest builders of all human history."[28]

> Then in 22 BC, he summoned a national assembly and announced his life-work the rebuilding of the Temple, on a magnificent scale, exceeding even the glory of Solomon's. The next two years were spent assembling and training a force of 10,000 workmen and 1,000 supervisory priests, who also worked as builder-craftsmen in the forbidden areas...He took extraordinary care not to offend the religious scruples of the rigorists.[29]

For example Herod used un-hewn stones for the altar so they would be untouched by iron tools and he made efforts to curtain off the inner sanctuaries during construction so that the Gentiles would not be unorthodoxly looking upon holiness. Herod built on the old site of the temple, yet because the plain on Mount Moriah was not large enough for his grand plan, Herod sliced down the peak next to the temple mount and filled in the gaps with rubble, effectively increasing the Temple mount area to 35 acres, with a circumference of one mile! The outside of the new Temple was covered in gold and silver, and Josephus describes it as being "exceptionally white." Apparently its gleam in bright sunlight could be seen from miles away! In the setting sun it must have had the appearance of being on fire! The construction took place over 46 years, however the workmen were still crafting the finishing touches just before 70 AD when the Romans tore the whole thing down leaving not one stone left on another (as prophesied).

Most impressive is that Herod the Great paid for the massive Temple overhaul himself.

In a display of Herod's craziness and paranoia, some students saw an eagle that Herod had built into the Temple architecture and they destroyed it. Herod had them hunted down, chained and brought to his Jericho residence where he burned them alive!

Another time, as Herod aged, he heard from visiting men from the east that another king had been born and his birth had been told in the stars. Then in an act so similar to what the Pharaoh of Egypt did at Moses' birth time, Herod hunted down all the baby boys two years and younger in the region of Bethlehem and murdered them. This became known in history as the "Slaughter of the Innocents." (This was when Joseph was warned in a dream to take his wife Mary and young Jesus to a safe place in Egypt.)

Herod's paranoid tendencies followed him always, even in relationship to his sons. When he discovered that one son (Antipater) attempted to poison him, Herod began to set things up for his own unavoidable demise by drafting a new will a mere four days before his death.[30] Herod, probably in

> the fear of dire consequences in leaving the whole kingdom in the hands of his youngest son, Herod divided Judea into several districts, and in his last will (about 4 B.C.) bequeathed to Antipas nothing but the tetrarchy of Galilee and Perea, which brought its ruler an income of 200 talents; giving to another son by Malthace, Archelaus, the right to the title of "king of Judea." Antipas did not acquiesce in this new partition of his father's dominions. He went to Rome, accompanied by the rhetorician Ireneus, and claimed the kingdom in accordance with Herod's earlier will; but though a deputation of fifty Jews had reached the imperial court to plead against Archelaus—and incidentally against Antipas—Augustus ratified the terms of the last will. [31]

Herod the Great "died in a most dramatic fashion. Josephus states that a loathsome disease descended upon the ruler as a judgment from God on account of his sins. He describes the horrible details—burning fever, ulcerated entrails, foul discharges, convulsions, stench, etc."[32]

When Herod died in 4 BC of what was probably intestinal cancer, his sons went nuts each claiming the right to succeed him in power. When none of them was the obvious victor, they ran to Caesar Augustus in Rome to settle their "argument." The Jews sent 50 representatives, as well, to beg for leadership from Caesar Augustus that was not like Herod. Augustus settled their disputes, kind of, and split the area into three parts. While the rulers were gone though, many disputes broke out.

> The people, worked up almost into a state of frenzy by the massacres brought about by Herod and Archelaus,

broke into open revolt in the absence of their ruler. The actual outbreak was without doubt directly caused by Sabinus—the procurator appointed by Augustus to assume charge pending the settlement of the succession—owing to his merciless oppression of the people. On the day of Pentecost in the year 4 B.C., a collision took place in the Temple precincts between the troops of Sabinus and the populace. Sabinus utilized his initial success in dispersing the people by proceeding to rob the Temple treasury. But disorders broke out all over the province, and his forces were not sufficient to repress them...What the loss on the Jewish side must have been may perhaps be surmised from the rabbinical tradition that the outbreak under Varus was one of the most terrible in Jewish history. [30]

Archelaus was allowed to rule for 10 years before he was called to Rome and his crown taken back.

The division of the Land[33] among Herod's three sons:

1. Herod Antipas: Tetrarch of Galilee and east bank of Jordan River
2. Philip: Tetrarch of the north east area called The Golan Heights
3. Archelaus: Ethnarch (national leader) of Samaria and Judaea.

These boys of Herod were not good news and things were definitely not hunky-dory in Judea. Living under Roman rule as a conquered people required payment of high taxes, and obedience to the whims of those in power, even to laws which promoted inequality such as described in the Bible when Jesus tells his followers that when they are conscripted to carry a soldier's pack for a mile, to walk with the man two miles. (Matt 5:41)

Though only governor of two small provinces, Antipas locally styled himself "king" & used the name "Herod," to bolster his claim that he was the true heir to his father's legacy. With the aid of Roman armies he crushed Galilean rebels & then turned to urbanizing southern Galilee, rebuilding the regional capitol [Sepphoris] that the Romans had destroyed in the civil

77

war & dedicating it to the emperor Augustus [calling it *Autocratoris:* "the Emperor's city"].[34]

The worst of the sons was Herod Archelaus. "He did much to accelerate the ultimate overthrow of Judean independence"[30] Matthew 2:22-23 describes Joseph's reaction in Egypt when he heard that Archelaus was in power.

> But when he heard that Archelaus was reigning in Judea in place of his father Herod, he was afraid to go there. Having been warned in a dream, he withdrew to the district of Galilee, and he went and lived in a town called Nazareth. So was fulfilled what was said through the prophets: "He will be called a Nazarene."

Archelaus acted as if he was for the good of the people in the earliest days, but would turn around and do things, it seemed, just to enrage the Jews. He once divorced his wife and married Glaphyra, the wife of his half-brother.

> This outraged the Jews, and when a rebellion broke out in Jerusalem during the Passover season, his troops killed over 3000 Jews. His was a reign of terror. In the ninth year of his reign, a delegation of leading men from Judea and Samaria went to Rome to appeal to Augustus to have him removed. Augustus agreed to their demands and removed Herod Archelaus. He also confiscated his fortune and banished him to Gaul.[35]

And later, "Like all of the rest (of the Herods), Herod Agrippa had a very high opinion of himself until one day, about 44 AD, he went too far: he, in effect, claimed to be divine (Acts 12:21-22)."Immediately an angel of The Lord smote him, because he did not give God the glory; and he was eaten by worms and died" (Acts 12:23 RSV).[36]

Enter Jesus the Messiah

It was into this societal mess of Hellenistic religious ways planting themselves into Judaism, Roman control, and Greek thought and language that Jesus the (long-awaited) Messiah was born. Joseph was warned in a dream to take Mary and the Child to Egypt in order to spare His life. Matt 2:13-15:

> When they had gone, an angel of the Lord appeared to Joseph in a dream. "Get up," he said, "take the child and his mother and escape to Egypt. Stay there until I tell you, for Herod is going to search for the child to kill him." So he got up, took the child and his mother during the night and left for Egypt, where he stayed until the death of Herod.

This travel fulfilled the prophecy from Hosea 11:1: Out of Egypt I called my Son.

What were the Jews looking for? There were so many varied prophecies over the centuries about the long-awaited Savior. The Jews constantly searched for him. The rabbis studied the holy texts trying to nail it down. I am sure their fervor is comparable to modern day Christian eschatologists (end times studiers).

Sadly, I am sure we will have misinterpreted some of the details in our search for Jesus' return when He appears as the historic Jews did when they missed His first visit. (Anyone remember the book *88 Reasons Why the Rapture will be in 1988?*)

Messianic Prophecies

According to various prophecies the Messiah was supposed to be from Galilee, Bethlehem, Nazareth, and Egypt! How does that come about? Did all but one have to be wrong? Nothing is impossible with God. We should never underestimate Him! Jesus fulfilled all these ancient and hardly reconcilable prophecies.

There are approximately 300 specifics recorded about the Messiah that God revealed to His people through the prophets so that Israel would recognize God's fulfillment of the ancient covenant promise to reconcile man to His heart. All of their asking for God to send Messiah had come to a culmination, a fulfillment, a promise kept, their longing had been satisfied. Unfortunately some wires got crossed. What the Jews had really been asking for was to be saved from their miserable circumstances. They were not looking for a Messiah who would call their sin "sin" and challenge them beyond the letter of the Law, to submit their hearts and motivations to God. And as a whole people/nation they were not interested.

But some were!

And God began to implement His bigger picture for redemption. One that invited all Mankind to come "home" to His heart.

A beautiful and fairly full covering of the scriptures prophesying the Messiah can be found at the Biblical Prophecy Research Center online[37] if you want to study this more completely. Here are some highlights:

Old Testament reference	Prophecy description	Fulfillment description	New Testament reference
Gen 12:3, 17:19, 21:12, 28:14, 49:10 II Sam 7:12-14	**Lineage** through Abraham, Isaac & Jacob, Judah & King David	Jesus' generation by generation lineage on both mother and earthly father's side traces to King David and Abraham	Matthew 1; Luke 3:33-34
Isa 9:6-7, Jer 23:5	Will inherit **David's throne**	Jesus is a descendant of David, & "King of the Jews"	Matt1:1, 1:6, Luke 3:33, Rom 1:3-4, Jn 19:19
Ps 110:4	Be a **Priest**	Former Pharisee Paul describes Jesus as Melchizedek.	Heb 5:5-6, 6:20, 7:15-17
Zach 9:9	Will enter Jerusalem on a **donkey**	Jesus enters Jerusalem on a never-ridden donkey at Triumphal entry.	Matt 21:1-11, Mark 11:1-11, Jn 12:12-16

Malachi 3:1	Enter the **Temple** with authority	Jesus clears the Temple of the moneychangers	Matt 21:12, Jn 2:13-22
Isa 7:14	Born of a virgin	Mary was a virgin when Jesus was born	Matt1:18-2:1, Luke 1:26-35
Zech 12:10, Ps 22:16	Will be pierced	A death unusual for Jews before the Romans, Jesus' pierced hands and feet verified by disciples' inspection	Matt 27:35, Jn 19:18, Luke 24:39, Jn 19:34-37
Ex 12:46, Ps 34:20	Bones unbroken like the Passover lamb	No bone in Jesus' body was broken. He was the final Passover lamb offering & died that day	Jn 19:33-36
Ps 16:10, Isa 53:9, Ps 2:7	Will be raised from the dead	Jesus was raised from the dead after 3 days	Matt 28:1-20, Acts 2:23-36, 7:55
Ps 41:9, 55:12-24, Zech 11:12	Be betrayed by a friend & for 30 pieces of silver	Judas, Jesus' disciple & friend gave Him up to the priests for 30 pieces of silver	Matt 26:21-25, 47-50; Jn 13:18-21; Acts 1:16-18, Matt 26:16
Isa 53:2, 63:3; Ps 69:8	Messiah rejected by His own people	Some of the Jews of Jesus' day rejected him, & begged for his crucifixion	Mark 6:3; Luke 9:58; Jn 1:11,

This is obviously not an exhaustive list, just a sampling. Most Christians I have interacted with all wonder with so many prophecies fulfilled so exactly through Jesus, how can the Jews "not see" and accept Jesus as their coming Messiah? Let's withhold our judgments by realizing first we have the HUGE advantage of hindsight. There are scriptures that we point to as being Messianic in nature, especially in Psalms, that we only see as descriptive of Jesus, BECAUSE we believe that Jesus is the Messiah. The Jews do not consider them "prophetic." They are poetry.

In addition, according to a conversation I once had with an orthodox rabbi who prefers to remain nameless, the biggest hold up is the Isaiah 53 description of the Messiah as a conquering king. Jesus certainly did not sweep into Jerusalem as an all-powerful, send-the-Roman-boots-quaking personality who deposed the cruelty of the Roman occupiers of the Holy Land that had been given to the Jews as the chosen people. In fact the people who sang "hosanna" waving palm branched as Jesus rode into Jerusalem on the previously un-ridden donkey thought that the conquering king was what they were getting. Hosanna means "save now," and the waving of palm branches was an ancient symbolic gesture of triumph and victory for the Jews. It had been used by the Maccabees when they came and relieved Jerusalem of her captors.

The triumphal entry and the palm branches were like the celebration of Jewish liberation in *1 Maccabees 13:51*:

> On the twenty-third day of the second month, in the one hundred and seventy-first year, the Jews [led by Simon Maccabeus] entered it [the fortress of Jerusalem] with praise and palm branches and with harps and cymbals and stringed instruments and with hymns and songs, because a great enemy had been crushed and removed from Israel.

> The *great enemy* in Jesus' days on earth was the Roman army; and one can imagine that many Jews saw the Triumphal Entry into Jerusalem as the advent of a revengeful Messiah who will wipe out the Romans from Holy Land. [38]

Though they "chose" Jesus as their Messiah and saving king on that day, when the Romans put Him to death on the cross, in their thinking, Jesus could not be the awaited "conquering king." He had been defeated. His defeat then, of course, called for them to reject Him as a "false messiah" to keep themselves pure for the Holy God, Yahweh.

Daniel even specifies that the coming Messiah would be rejected by His own people BEFORE the destruction of the second Temple.

> Know and understand this: From the issuing of the decree to restore and rebuild Jerusalem until the Anointed One, the ruler, comes, there will be seven 'sevens,' and sixty-two 'sevens.' It will be rebuilt with streets and a trench, but in times of trouble. After the sixty-two 'sevens,' the Anointed One will be cut off and will have nothing. The people of the ruler who will come will destroy the city and the sanctuary. The end will come like a flood: War will continue until the end, and desolations have been decreed. (Daniel 9:25-26).

Daniel said these inspired words before the second temple even existed, or had been subjected to Herod's grand modification. The second Temple was destroyed by the Romans in 70 AD, about 35-40 years after Jesus was put to death—the ultimate "rejection by his own people." To this day, the Temple has not been rebuilt. [However all the furnishings, the lamp stands, tables, utensils etc, are made according to the ancient Biblical instructions and ready to be moved in. One of the gigantic menorahs (lamp stands) is on display a few hundred meters from the Western Wall in Jerusalem.]

But God knew all of this ahead of time, and chose to send His son, Jesus, anyway, as a way to reconcile even the Gentiles unto Himself, if they only believe He is God and accept that His death and resurrection is the punishment of their sins. (Thank you for your far-sighted kindness, Yahweh!)

The following prophetic description of the coming Messiah found in Isaiah 9:6-7 is one of the scriptures that causes Jews to reject Jesus as fulfilling the signs.

> For to us a child is born, to us a son is given, and the government will be on his shoulders. And he will be called Wonderful Counselor, Mighty God, Everlasting Father, Prince of Peace. Of the increase of his govern-

ment and peace there will be no end. He will reign on David's throne and over his kingdom, establishing and upholding it with justice and righteousness from that time on and forever. The zeal of the LORD Almighty will accomplish this.

Jesus, when he lived on earth, did not take up David's Jerusalem throne, overthrow the Roman rule and "set things right" as the Jews had hoped and prayed for over the centuries. Instead, Jesus established a new heavenly Kingdom in which people become the Temple and He sits on the throne of our hearts, where the daily sacrifice is our obedience and slaying of our will in favor of God's will, where the priestly garment of righteousness can be worn by all believers, and we are adorned by the fruit of the Spirit as we represent our great Messiah King. His Kingdom is everlasting and always expanding, from Jerusalem, to Judea and Samaria to the ends of the earth!

Messiah vs Christ- A note so that you can correctly use terms. *Messiah* and *Christ* are the same word. *Christ* is not Jesus' last name. They both mean "anointed One." *Messiah* is the Anglicized version of the Hebrew word that is transliterated *mashiac*, and *Christ* is the Greek word for the idea of a *mashiac*. So to say "Jesus Christ the Messiah" is redundant and means "Jesus anointed one anointed one." Use of either one or the other is correct, just not both. And now you are in the know.

Note on the Roman Occupiers-Just as in modern times of occupation, the Roman occupiers of Judea were not all horrible warmongers, bent on power, abusive authority, and destruction; and they were not all kind and generous either. Take for example a story described by Luke. When a Roman officer in Capernaum (in the Galilee) had a highly valued slave who was sick and nearly dead, he called on some highly respected Jewish leaders to bring Jesus to heal his slave. The Jews said of the Roman officer, "If anyone deserves your help, it is he...he loves the Jews and even built a synagogue for us." Then the officer sent some friends to tell Jesus that he understood His authority, that he did not feel worthy of Jesus coming into his home, and asked Jesus to heal his slave from afar. Jesus said of the officer to the crowd following him, "I haven't seen faith like this in all the land of Israel." When the officer's friends arrived home, the slave had been healed. (Luke 7:1-10).

This story illustrates that

- there were some respectful occupiers
- they understood Jesus' authority (both the officer & his friends who obeyed him and obeyed Jesus)
- they understood their own authority.
- there was good relationship between some occupying officers and the Jews

Matthew 9:18 describes a ruler coming and kneeling before Jesus and begging him to heal his daughter. The girl had died, and Jesus raised her from the dead. This story illustrates much of the same as the first one. The ruler would have been an occupier, and yet he knew enough of Jesus to honor Him and to ask for healing for his daughter.

CHAPTER 7

LESSON: THE DESTRUCTION OF JUDEA

Topics: Temple Destruction, 9th of Av, Masada & map, Palestine, Diaspora, where did they go? the wandering, persecuted Jew, Renaming of Judea and Jerusalem.

Daniel prophesied it, Ezekiel prophesied it, Jeremiah prophesied it, even Jesus prophesied it. The great temple of Herod in Jerusalem would be destroyed, and Abraham's children scattered over the face of the earth because they did not remain faithful to Yahweh. Yet even in the scattering there was an element of mercy. God was being faithful to His covenant, yes. But He also knew that in the scattering, His people would call on His name. They would search for Him. They always did in hardship. In addition, the scattering caused Abraham's children to remember the traditions passed down and hold them as sacred. They brought those traditions into every society where they lived, thus spreading the name of Yahweh far and wide. Keep in mind that some of those scattered Jews were also believers in Jesus, and the fame of Jesus abounded. It is possible that had the scattering of the Jews not taken place as is did, that Christianity might have died out as just another religious sect of Judaism.

Even 40 years after Jesus' ascension back into heaven, when Rome had been controlling Judea for about 120 years, all the troubles being endured by the Jews had not stopped. The disciples and Paul were spreading the good news of God's desire to be reconciled with man through the Messiah Whom He had sent to earth, and it was being widely accepted—outside of Judea. Inside of Judea there were more uprisings, rebellions. Most often the Jews were rising up against the outrageous taxation and the corruption in the Temple.

The Roman Emperor Caligula was one of the major prods that encouraged even moderate Jews to join with the Zealots who had been instigating the rebellions for quite some time already. Caligula declared himself to be god around 32 AD and demanded his statue to be worshiped throughout the empire. The Jews refused! It is thought that they were not massacred at this point only because Caligula suffered a very fast and awful demise as soon as he made his declaration. God has a thing about man (or Satan) trying to usurp His glory, or His name. "Caligula's sudden demise might also have been interpreted as confirming the Zealots' belief that God would fight alongside the Jews if only they would have the courage to confront Rome."[39]

In 66 AD the last Roman ruler in Judea, Florus, stole mass quantities of silver from the Temple. The outraged Jews rose up in what became known as the Great Revolt and wiped out the Roman garrison that was stationed in Jerusalem. When Syria's Roman ruler, Celestus Gallus sent reinforcements, the more-than-excited Jews dismantled Gallus's forces too. The Jews became convinced that they could overthrow Rome itself. However, that was their last decisive victory.

> When the Romans returned, they had 60,000 heavily armed and highly professional troops. They launched their first attack against the Jewish state's most radicalized area, the Galilee in the north. The Romans vanquished the Galilee, and an estimated 100,000 Jews were killed or sold into slavery.[39]

And the Galilee squashing was just the beginning. The Roman troops swept south toward Jerusalem. But a few escapee Jews preceded them. When the radical refugees arrived in Jerusalem they began to kill any Jewish leaders who were not as radical as they were. Between 66 and 68 AD, all the moderate Jewish leaders were killed off, and not by the Romans, by their own Jewish brothers.[39]

So while the Jews were killing each other inside the walled city, the Romans were building their encampment outside the walls and preparing to wage a siege against the city.

> While the Romans would have won the war in any case, the Jewish civil war both hastened their victory and immensely increased the casualties. One horrendous example: In expectation of a Roman siege, Jerusalem's Jews had stockpiled a supply of dry food that could have fed the city for many years. But one of the warring Zealot factions burned the entire supply,

The Romans breached Jerusalem's walls in the summer of 70 AD, and
the fall of Judea was clenched.

The 9th of Av, 70 AD marks another major blow to the Jews. On the very
anniversary of the destruction of the first temple, (Solomon's Temple),
the second temple was set ablaze as the Romans, led by Titus. This
destruction fulfilled the ancient and not-so-ancient words of the prophets:
"Not one stone shall be left on another" (Mark 13:2).

As the siege continued all the trees that had once adorned Judea, and its
capital, Jerusalem, were hacked down to be used as firewood for the
impending army and to build their war implements, ladders, and siege
towers.

> No one - not even a foreigner - who had seen the Old
> Judea and the glorious suburbs of the City, and now
> set eyes on her present desolation, could have helped
> sighing and groaning at so terrible a change; for every
> trace of beauty had been blotted out by war.[40]

Accompanying Titus was an historian, Flavius Josephus. He recorded,
after the fact, the details of the events that destroyed Jerusalem. The
bodies of the dead were stacked "like cordwood" when the Romans
breached the gates of the city. Titus had given orders NOT to destroy the
temple, but the Roman soldiers were angry that they had to suffer
through the summer heat because the Jews refused to surrender. So, the
soldiers set fire to the beloved temple against orders.

Herod's Temple

We have only touched on what the temple would have looked like. The
sheer size of the place was monstrous. A mountain top had been cleared
to make space for all the colonnades and porches and connecting
stairways that Herod added. There were courtyards for the public, inner

courts for Jews only, the court of the women, courtyards closer to the Holy of Holies for Jewish men only, places for sacrifices, and for the multitudes required to be present at the Feasts of the Lord 3-4 times a year: perhaps upwards of a million people. The temple itself was crowned with hammered gold over the stone adornment, with two gigantic columns flanking each side of the entrance. Stunning. Even compared to what the Roman soldiers might have seen in Rome, the temple was splendid. The yard is estimated at 35 acres, larger certainly than some entire villages of the time. This temple was magnificent!

The gold and silver both of the city and the temple treasury, plus the temple implements (i.e. massive candlesticks/lamp stands, knives, incense burners, bowls, water and oil vessels, etc.) had been stored in the temple for safekeeping. When the fire spread, the gold and silver began to melt. The walls had been plated in gold too, courtesy of Herod the Great. The soldiers gathered up all of it, and when it ran down into the cracks of the walls, they upturned the gigantic rocks that made up the temple walls to get at the gold. Thus the soldiers fulfilled Jesus' words that no stone will be left upon another.

"While the Temple was on fire and there was tremendous looting, killing and rape many rushed to the Temple to die rather than become Roman slaves."[41] The Menorahs and other sacred objects that had not melted down were carried off to Rome as spoils of war. A tour guide I had once pointed out that the Coliseum in Rome was built immediately after Titus's soldiers returned to Rome from looting Jerusalem's holy temple, and could have very easily been financed by the gold stolen from the Jews' temple treasury and walls. However, there is no empirical evidence to support this theory.

According to Josephus, the mourning and wailing of the Jews could be heard over the roar of the fire that swept over the temple, and tears filled the eyes of the Romans who stood watching from the south hill where their garrison was located. (Incidentally the hill that the Romans chose to build on was locally known as the Hill of Bad Advice. After they left the area, it remained empty for 18 centuries. Then the UN moved into Jerusalem and lo and behold, they found a perfect hill to build their station for peacekeeping. Cough* cough* it's the same hill!)

> As the flames went upward, the Jews made a great
> clamour, such as so mighty an affliction required, and
> ran together to prevent it; and now they spared not
> their lives any longer, nor suffered anything to restrain
> their force, since that holy house was perishing . . .
> thus it was the holy house burnt down . . . Nor can one
> imagine any thing greater or more terrible than this
> noise; for there was at once a shout of the Roman
> Legions, who were marching all together, and a sad
> clamour of the seditious, who were now surrounded
> with fire and sword . . . the people under a great
> consternation, made sad moans at the calamity they
> were under . . . Yet was the misery itself more terrible
> than this disorder; for one would have thought that the
> hill itself, on which the Temple stood, was seething
> hot, as full of fire on every part of it.[42]

The destruction of Jerusalem in 70 AD, culminating with the burning of
the Temple is said to be one of the most devastating ever. According to
Josephus, "we may sum it up by saying that no other city has ever
endured such horrors."[43]

History of the 9th of Av. The devastation that occurred on the 9th of Av
in Jerusalem in 70 AD, was not the first such tragedy to befall the Jews
on this date. In fact, it seems like the worst of trouble seems to always
fall on this date, as if they are still being punished for their first sin
associated with the Promised Land. When the Israelites first crossed over
the Jordan River and sent the spies into the Land to scope it out, and 40
days later they came back with the report, the Israelites believed the bad
report of the 10 spies. They did not trust that God was big enough to
conquer the people who were there already.

The day the Israelites first chose not to believe God was the 9th of Av. In
trying to root out the unbelief in God's love for them, He led them
through 40 years of wandering in the wilderness until all the unbelievers
of that generation were dead, buried in the desert of their unbelief.

The 9th of Av

The following Jewish tragedies have all occurred on the same Hebrew
calendar day, the 9th of Av:

- **Spies' Bad report,**—which caused 40 years of wandering in the desert before entering the Promised Land.
- **Solomon's Temple, 586 BC**—Nebuchadnezzar destroyed the first temple and took Judah captive to Babylon.
- **The Second Temple, 70 AD**— Titus's men sacked the great Temple build by Herod, stole the gold and sent most of the surviving population of Jerusalem scattering for 2000 years.
- **Jerusalem Plowed, 130 AD**—Emperor Hadrian ordered Jerusalem to be plowed in preparation for building new pagan city, "Aelia Capitolina," on the location, fulfilling Micah 3:12 and Jeremiah 26:18. Hadrian changed the name of Judea to "Palaestina."[41]
- **Fall of Betar, 133 AD**— the last stronghold in the heroic Bar Kochba rebellion, fell to the Romans after a three-year siege. 580,000 Jews died by starvation or the sword. [42]
- **Expelled from England, 1290** by King Edward I.
- **Spanish Inquisition, 1492** was sanctioned by King Ferdinand and Queen Isabella on the 9th of Av, ending many centuries of flourishing Jewish life in Spain. Called the Alhambra Decree.
- **Vienna Expulsion, 1670** the last of the Jews fled Vienna on the 9th of Av this year.
- **World War I, 1914** Germany invaded Russia sparking off WWI on the 9th of Av.
- **Final Solution, 1940.** Himmler presented his "Final Solution" to the Jewish problem to the Nazi party on the 9th of Av.
- **Warsaw Ghetto, 1942**—the Nazi's began deporting the Jews from the Warsaw Ghetto on the 9th of Av.
- **Gush Katif, 2006**—residents of this Israeli township were ousted from their homes by their own IDF soldiers who cried at having to do it in order to try to bring about peace in Gaza, just one day after the 9th of Av (so as NOT to coincide with the holiday)

The 9th of Av (*Tisha b'Av*) is remembered by Jews every year by mourning and fasting.

Masada, 73 AD. As the Romans sacked Jerusalem in 70 AD there was a stronghold about 30 miles south where several hundred men, women and children had been holed up. They occupied one of Herod the Great's former castles across from the Dead Sea, called Masada. Herod, as usual, designed this palace fortress—more like a small city—on a grand scale. It was his desert spa. A sect of the Zealots called the Sicarii had overcome the Roman garrison who guarded this fortress in 66 AD, and had moved in to use it as a base for running raids on nearby and not-so-nearby towns. As with most things Jewish, there was a split opinion. Some of the families were there wanting to live lives wholly consecrated to God; others were the ones planning and carrying out raids, led by Elazar ben Ya'ir. By the time Jerusalem had been destroyed there were about 900 Jews living in Masada.[44] Masada was carved into and on top of a mountain in the desert wilderness and was easily defensible because of its grand height (1300 feet on the east, 300 feet on the west). Not only was the palace on top of a mountain, but it was surrounded with a massive casement wall that any enemy who managed to scale the mountain then had to deal with.[44]

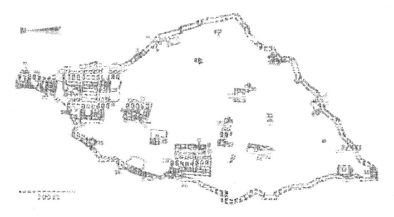

Map of Masada:[44] 1. snake path gate. 2. rebel dwellings. 3. Byzantine monastic cave. 4. eastern water cistern. 5. rebel dwellings. 6. mikvah. 7. southern gate. 8. rebel dwellings. 9. southern water cistern. 10. southern fort. 11. swimming pool. 12. small palace. 13. round columbarium tower. 14. mosaic workshop. 15. small palace. 16. small palace. 17. public immersion pool. **18-21. Western Palace:** 18. service area. 19. residential area. 20. storerooms. 21. administrative area. 22. tanners' tower 23. western Byzantine gate. 24. columbarium towers. 25. synagogue 26. Byzantine church. 27. barracks. **28-39. Northen Palace:** 28. grand residence. 29. quarry. 30. commandant's headquarters 31. tower. 32. administration building. 33. gate. 34. storerooms. 35. bathhouse. 36. water gate.

37-39. Herod's Palace: 37. upper terrace. 38. middle terrace. 39. lower terrace. A. ostraca cache found in casemate. B. Herod's throne room. C. colorful mosaic. D. Roman breaching point. E. coin cache found. F. ostraca cache found. G. three skeletons found.

The whole mountain top fortress measures approximately 1800 feet by 900 feet. That is just over 1/3 of a mile long! The walls contain room after room for storage of food and soldiers, originally. The 37,000 square foot, 3-tiered palace contained hot and cold bath houses, steam rooms with mosaic tile floors, a swimming pool and beautifully appointed royal apartments.[45] Masada could house thousands of soldiers, and it was fully stocked with food and enjoyed an elaborate system of channels that captured any rainfall for drinking and swimming water storage.

So, these families, at least part of them, had been living at Masada as a community for seven to eight years before the Romans decided to clear them out.

The Factions of Judaism

But who were these folks who had escaped Jerusalem and now resided at Masada? Judaism was fractioned into four basic groups with subdivisions in each one. (Sounds like pre-denominations to me). There were the Essenes, Sadducees, Pharisees, and Zealots. The Zealots were the most politically extreme group, while the Essenes were the most devout who separated themselves from Jewish society by living similarly to monks. The Zealots had an even more extreme group of men among them who were willing to risk death in order to infiltrate their enemies, and try to bring about change and freedom through striking back with violence. They were called the Sicarii. These were the "outlaws" residing in Masada and striking out on their missions/raids from there.

The taking of Masada was not a task any Roman commander in his right mind would volunteer for, because

- The few people holed up there were not important in the grand scheme of things, they were not doing major damage with their little raids to the nearby communities or army outposts.

- The Romans could hardly siege them out like a normal walled community. Courtesy of Herod's planning, the community was stocked with 10 times as much food as needed, because their numbers were 1/10 of the army Herod had planned to house there in time of trouble. And the Roman Army had no access to water. In the Judean Desert, that is a BIG problem.
- The commanders knew how impregnable Masada was, and no one wanted to risk the humiliation a loss would bring to his career (or possibly his life).

But the Romans had to save face and reputation as the mightiest army that ever was, and that was one of the main instigations in wiping out all the Jews' strongholds. So Flavius Silva finally took it on.

The only way to besiege this city was to hurry it up, so eight garrisons of Roman soldiers (about 10,000 men) surrounded the base of the mountain in their square camps. You can still see the wall remains of their encampments today. And once they put a supply chain into effect to bring food, water, and slaves into the desert, they began building a siege ramp up the shallowest side of the mountain (the back side if facing the Dead Sea). Only, instead of subjecting themselves to the Sicarii tossing boulders over the side of the mountain, it is said that the army forced the captured Jews from farther north, perhaps even Jerusalem, to build the ramp day after day in the heat, against their own brothers.[51] The Jews inside did not kill their fellow enslaved Jews, even though it brought about their own deaths more quickly.

The impending wall-breach at Masada went on for about 3 months. They must have known it was only a matter of time, yet, I am sure that up until the last minutes, they kept the hope that Yahweh would rescue them as His faithful followers, the way He had come through for them in ages past.

This story of the fall of Masada was told to Josephus by two surviving women and five children who hid themselves in cisterns and surrendered to the Roman Army when they breached the fortress:

In spring of 73 AD, the ramp had been completed and somehow the wooden barrier wall they had erected caught fire. I am sure these 966 souls could feel the inevitability of being surrounded by the mightiest army in the world with a path that led to their "door," yet hope and faith of a miracle must have danced in their hearts. The night before the Romans would invade the following morning, the Jewish leader, Elazar ben Ya'ir, brought the heads of the families together. They could not, they would not, be captured and become slaves to the wicked Roman idol-worshippers. They felt their very eternal souls were at risk. Judaism in all its various sects and divisions discouraged suicide. I would assume this is because the person's flesh is no longer alive to ask forgiveness and offer sacrifices.

They decided that the fathers would kill their wives and children that night, and then 10 men would kill the other men, and they drew lots to see who would kill the 10, leaving just one man who would kill himself.

The Jews left their massive food storage intact so it could never be said that the Roman Army conquered all the Jews. Then they put their plan into action. When the Romans swept over the casement walls the next day, and broke through the charred reinforcement wooden barrier, they found only corpses.

When Masada was rediscovered in 1842 (it was lost to history over 1700 years of earthquakes in a barren landscape) and excavations and rebuilding began in the 1960's, some interesting items were found.

There were 11 potshards containing Jewish names written in Hebrew. "One name, Ben Yair, seems to correspond to the name of the leader of the rebels in Masada, Eleazar ben Yair."[47] And in the Synagogue, two Biblical scrolls. Including Ezekiel 37. This section of scripture recounts God asking Ezekiel "can these dry bones live?" These faithful followers of Yahweh who gave up their very lives to keep from sinning against God by the force of the Romans, must have found comfort in these scriptures. Perhaps they even read this portion just before they died, holding on to faith, that God could indeed raise up their own dry bones into an army if He chose. The other scripture was from Deuteronomy, part of which describes lifestyle God expected of Israel.[48]

The following description is given by the literature distributed at Masada National Park:

The rebels lived mainly in rooms in the casement walls, as attested by stoves, niches for food storage and other finds from daily life unearthed in them. Articles of clothing, baskets, household implements and other items were found in piles of ash, apparently burned intentionally by their owners so as not to fall into the hands of the enemy.

More than 5,000 coins were found at Masada, mostly minted by the rebels. Especially moving are the silver coins bearing the words "Shekel of Israel" and "Jerusalem the Holy," with letters indicating each of the five years of the rebellion. Portions of scrolls were uncovered, along with more than 700 ostraca (shards bearing inscriptions.

Hundreds of ballista balls fired at the fortress by the Romans and found atop the plateau attest to the heated battle between the rebels and the forces of their imperial enemy.[49]

When the new State of Israel affirmed their new soldiers into the IDF (Israeli Defense Forces) the ceremony would take place at Masada, and the cry would go out, "never again!" This tradition has been changed in recent years, but it attests to the significance of Masada in the Jewish psyche.

Except for the poorest of the poor, now slaves in their own land, the taking of Masada on 15th of Nisan 73 AD, ended Jewish life in Judea.

The renaming of Judea (Palestine) & Jerusalem (Aelia Capitolina).

Even though nearly 1.2 million Jews were killed or sold into slavery between 66 and 72 AD, the few who remained maintained hope that Jerusalem would be restored.[50] And they taught their children to hope for it. But a new city was built on top of the old site of Jerusalem and the Jews were not allowed to enter it, except one day a year to mourn the loss of their temple, and you guessed it: the 9th of Av.

In the first hundred years after the city and Temple were destroyed, there was high expectation among the Jews that they would once again return to their land and rebuild that which was devastated. The Court of 70 Elders, the Sanhedrin, was intact and many Jews still lived in small communities in Israel. Their hopes were dashed by the Emperor Hadrian when he decided to establish a new city on the ruins of Jerusalem. The Old City was plowed up to make way for the new Roman city to be named Colonia Aelia Capitolina.[41]

When Hadrian came in and rebuilt the city he decided that he would make it a place for legionnaires, and the Jews would never be allowed to return.[51] The new city was named after Hadrian himself. His family/clan name was "Aeilus," and "Capitolina" dedicated the new city to the god Jupiter Capitolinus.

Fundamentalist Jews were angry at Hadrian's harshness and began stowing away weapons for a revolt. Hadrian set up new temples to the Roman gods and regional gods, further incensing the Jews. The revolt was not long lived, but it enraged Hadrian and his harshness increased. He seemed to be determined to wipe Judea off the map (sound familiar to our current news reports of Iran's and the rest of the Middle East's leadership?). Hadrian renamed the province "Syria Paleastina."

The "Paleastina" bit of the name was derived from the ancient enemies of the Israelites those pesky Philistines who Israel had such trouble with over the years. It was a deliberate insult to the remaining Jews that they would be called after the name of their arch enemies, even though there were no more Philistines actually alive. This "Provincia Syria Paleastina" was shortened to "Paleastina" and over the years came to the modern pronunciation "Palestine." [52]

The name "Falastin" that Arabs today use for "Palestine" is not an Arabic name. It is the Arab pronunciation of the Roman "Palaestina". Quoting Golda Meir, former Prime Minister of Israel:

The British chose to call the land they mandated Palestine, and the Arabs picked it up as their nation's supposed ancient name, though they couldn't even pronounce it correctly and turned it into Falastin a fictional entity.[53]

The Diaspora's dispersion: Where did they go from Judea?

The Jews when they ran from Judea, or were carted off as property, have landed and launched new lives in every nation on the planet. To assimilate or not to assimilate? that is the everlasting question for the Jews. And for the most part they did both. Many Jews clung to their rituals of eating kosher and celebrating Shabbat and the Holy days. Some "lost" their Jewish differences so as to blend into the societies where they settled. To stand out invited persecution.

The concept of diaspora goes ever farther back. The word itself means dispersion. It originated in the Septuagint, one of the original Greek translations of the Bible, in Deuteronomy 28:25: "though shalt be a diaspora in all kingdoms of the earth." The Oxford English Dictionary cites the first English usage from the year 1876; and more recently, dozens of ethnic or national groups have appropriated the term to explain their own geographically scattered communities."[54]

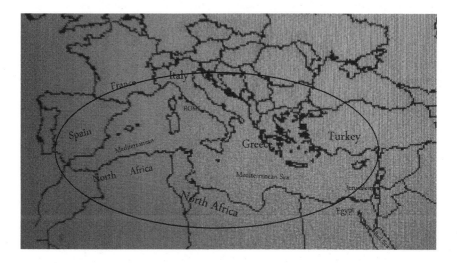

This map shows the first few centuries of dispersion The Jews settled themselves within the general area of the oval of dispersion

98

surrounding the Mediterranean Sea. The dispersion grew wider and longer, so the simple answer is that they went everywhere. Pockets of Jewish society popped up and, usually whenever they started to thrive, there would be persecution—miserable persecutions—and they would be forced out, farther and farther from their homeland. And they would settle in and start the cycle over again until they were dispersed all over Africa, the region of the Middle East, India, Eastern and Western Europe, and finally to the Americas. The greatest population of Jews today lives in North America. Of the 13 million Jews world wide in the 21st century, 6.5 million reside in the US.[56]

But the Lord promised that when the time of the Gentiles was complete, that He would whistle for His chosen people and they would come home. For 17, 18 centuries even, this seemed like it could only happen figuratively. However in our day, in our time, we are seeing God's promise fulfilled.

> **Isaiah 5:26** He lifts up a banner for the distant nations, he whistles for those at the ends of the earth. Here they come, swiftly and speedily!

> **Zachariah 10:6-10 (NKJV)** I will strengthen the house of Judah, and I will save the house of Joseph. I will bring them back, because I have mercy on them. They shall be as though I had not cast them aside; For I am the LORD their God, and I will hear them. Those of Ephraim shall be like a mighty man, And their heart shall rejoice as if with wine. Yes, their children shall see *it* and be glad; Their heart shall rejoice in the LORD. I will whistle for them and gather them, For I will redeem them; And they shall increase as they once increased. I will sow them among the peoples, And they shall remember Me in far countries; They shall live, together with their children, and they shall return. I will also bring them back from the land of Egypt, And gather them from Assyria. I will bring them into the land of Gilead and Lebanon, until no *more room* is found for them.

Can a nation be born in a day? Yes. May 14, 1948. The birth pains leading up to that day is our next topic.

CHAPTER 8

LESSON: THE BIRTH OF A NATION (IS. 66:8)

Topics: How did Israel again become a nation after so many centuries of exile from their homeland? And has it ever happened before in history? Dreyfuss Affair, Zionism, Weizmann, Holocaust Brief

Let's set the stage a moment. By the 1850's AD the Jews, God's chosen people have lived among the nations twice as long as they ever lived in the Promised Land of Israel. They have lived as the "scum of the earth" always persecuted, always hunted down. Those who should have been their closest allies, Christians, have been some of their fiercest enemies throughout the last 800 years, beginning with the Crusades, continuing through the Expulsion from England, and the morbid Spanish Inquisition.

After the Romans demolished civilization in the Promised Land it changed hands many times in the next two millennia. (A full list can be viewed in Chapter 10.) But it is not as if this particular chunk of land had any great beauty to be fought over or any massive trade route crossroads to be desirable. (There was a trade route intersection, but they could have easily rerouted). When the Ottomans ruled the area (1800's), they had a brilliant idea of taxing a property by the number of trees it contained. As with people of every day and age, the inhabitants were looking for a way to lower their tax dues. So they chopped down their trees, both forests of trees and trees in their front yards. The Land, once called "a land flowing with milk and honey," was stripped bare. The lack of trees gave the soil over to erosion and interrupted normal rainfall cycles causing even more desolation. Mark Twain visited the Holy Land in 1867 and wrote about his experience in a book called *Innocents Abroad*.

> "..... A desolate country whose soil is rich enough, but is given over wholly to weeds... a silent mournful expanse.... a desolation.... we never saw a human being on the whole route.... hardly a tree or shrub anywhere. Even the olive tree and the cactus, those fast friends of a worthless soil, had almost deserted the country"[57]

Herman Melville (American author of *Moby Dick*) describes Jerusalem as this:

> "Wandering among the tombs-till I began to think myself one of those possessed with devils...The color of the whole city is gray and looks at you like a cold gray eye in a cold old man-its strange aspect in the pale olive light of the morning."[58]

What is it that gives this land such great value that everyone wants it now? Again we see how Satan wants whatever belongs to God. Whether it is the worship and glory of heaven that belongs to God, the people—both Jews and Christians, or the Land called Israel which God states in Psalm 24:1 is HIS. It belongs to Him and He has given it to the Jews as a permanent possession. (I suppose considering its state of decline in the 1800's, Israel did not look like too exciting a prospect).

> Psalm 24:1: The earth is the LORD's, and everything in it, the world, and all who live in it;

> Genesis 17:7-8 I will establish my covenant as an everlasting covenant between me and you and your descendants after you for the generations to come, to be your God and the God of your descendants after you. The whole land of Canaan, where you are now an alien, I will give as an everlasting possession to you and your descendants after you; and I will be their God" (emphasis mine).

So after the Jews endured 18 centuries of exile from Israel, the following is the chain of events God used to stir the pot of world history toward His plan of bringing His people home to the Land where He promised to bring them back from exile. Here is how He started:

Alfred Dreyfus Affair
France defeated the Prussians in 1870-1871 which brought into France a huge nationalistic spirit, a love of the army, and a suspicion over foreign nationals and foreigners in general, but the French culture also fostered anti-Semitism because Jews were viewed as "French pretenders." Much of the population became obsessed with revenge too. The power of

government kept flopping left then right and then left again. In a word, France was unstable.

In 1894, some reports that should not have been there were found in a wastepaper basket. They were sent away for a handwriting analysis, but before the report even came back, they had decided on their spy: Alfred Dreyfus, a Jewish man who served as a French Army Intelligence officer. He was the only Jew on staff. Dreyfus was suspected because of his yearly visits to his family back in Germany (and extreme levels of anti-Semitism high up in the French Army).

October 15, 1894, Dreyfus was arrested for espionage, and they held an unusual and super secret courts martial. However, when he was pronounced guilty, Dreyfus was publically stripped of his army rank and shipped off to prison on Devil's Island in French Guiana. This courts martial violated proper procedure and the whole affair became the basis for agitation between the left and right governments and anti-Semitic people in France. During a particular rally, the mob could be heard screaming, "Death to the Jews!"[59]

Well, when a new leader in French Military Intelligence came into power, Lt Col Piquart, he looked into the evidence against Dreyfus, and found that the real traitor was actually Major Esterhazy. When Piquart tried to make public the injustice and get Dreyfus a new trial, Piquart was transferred to the Sahara Desert south of Tunisia! But word did leak to the press of an army cover up. By 1898, (Dreyfus had been in prison on Devil's Island for 4 years!) some celebrities got on board with kicking up a fuss over the injustice.

Once the press got involved, it was proven (and later proven in court) that Lt Col Sandherr and some associates actually manufactured and forged the papers and other evidence against Dreyfus. They had been encouraged by the Minister of War, General Auguste Mercier![59]

One of the men in the press fighting for Dreyfus was Emile Zola who had published in a newspaper a famous open letter to the President of France, Félix Faure. It was considered inflammatory, (which was Zola's point!) and he was tried for libel. Zola was convicted and ran to England on the advice of his lawyers. But Zola's sacrifice set things in motion in

France. The next president, Emile Loubet, allowed Dreyfus to come home, pardoned, in September 1899. However it was not until 1906 that Dreyfus was exonerated and given back his military commission. "During World War I, Dreyfus came out of retirement and volunteered to serve as a lieutenant-colonel. Though past retirement age, Dreyfus served in the front-line in 1917. Finally, Lt Colonel Dreyfus was granted the rank of Officer of the Legion of Honor in November 1918."[59]

And how does the Dreyfus Cover-Up differ from all the other anti-Semitic events that have occurred over and over throughout history? Actually, not a lot, it just happened to be the spark that lit the fire that finally caught and spread because the conditions were finally right. (Meaning it was God's timing!) However, first we need to talk about Zionism.

Zionism
A prevailing feeling among some Jews of high intelligence and some influence scattered through Europe was a desire to have a homeland of their own. The Nationalist Movement (pride in your own nation and in belonging to your nationality) was going on worldwide, and at the same time there was a growing awareness that Judaism was more than just a religion. It had morphed into an identity of history, shared ideology, tradition, and religion. Yet Jews were politically without power because they were scattered among the nations.

This combination of worldwide nationalism growth and the realization that Jewishness was both religion and blood, cultivated rich earth for the planting of the Zionist movement. As interest spread among the Jews of Europe, several prominent men rose above the others. Among them were the men for whom the streets of Israel are now named: ben Yahuda, Pinsker, ben Gurion, Herzl, Weizmann, Jabotinsky, etc. It was not smooth sailing into statehood as soon as the idea cropped up. As with most things Jewish, for every two Jews there were three opinions. Even on where the homeland should be located: at that time the leaders considered locations within Argentina, Uganda, and the site of ancient Judea and Israel as viable options.

In the beginning growing pains of Zionism, Theodor Herzl rose to leadership. He describes a new Israel as a socialist Utopia in his novel

Altneuland (translated as "Old New Land") published in 1902. Apparently, it gave words to the heart longings of the Jewish masses. Herzl appealed to prominent and wealthy Jews such as Baron Rothschild and Baron Hirsch to invest in a new Jewish homeland in Israel, but without success. So Herzl turned to the Jewish masses in Europe. The resulting meeting and sharing of ideas August 29-31, 1897 in Switzerland was called the First Zionist Congress.

The Zionist movement's connection to the Dreyfus Affair is one that is familiar to readers of the New Testament's description of the Apostle Paul being present at Stephen's martyrdom (Acts 6-7). Theodor Herzl witnessed the mobs shouting "death to the Jews" in France during the events surrounding Alfred Dreyfus. He decided then and there to dedicate his life to bringing about a homeland where Jews could be Jews and be respected for it. Assimilation was NOT working and something had to be done.

The First Zionist Congress was gathered in Basle, Switzerland in 1897, and was organized by Herzl. (Originally slated for Munich, Germany, public outcry by both Orthodox and Reform Jews, caused a shift in venues.) But the Congress was not at all religiously based. It was the first inter-territorial gathering of Jews as a "pre-nation," but it was secular in its outlook. About 200 people attended. The delegates accomplished several things[60] at this meeting:
1. They adopted the "Basle Program" as the program of the Zionist Movement. The program declares, "Zionism seeks to establish a home for the Jewish people in Palestine secured under public law"
2. They formed the World Zionist Organization as the public arm of this movement
3. They elected Theodor Herzl as president of this new organization

Herzl wrote in his diary after this first meeting, "At Basle, I founded the Jewish state. If not in five years, then certainly in fifty, everyone will realize it." And it was only a few months more than 50 years later, in May 1948, that Herzl's words came true. Israel became a nation state in her own right. Unfortunately, those 50 years were the most devastating to worldwide Jewry as all the previous years of prejudice, hate, exile, and murder combined.

Sadly, Herzl had not lived to see the day. He died at age 44 in 1904, just seven years after the First Zionist Congress. But Herzl's "name has been commemorated in the Herzl Forests at Ben Shemen and Hulda, the world's first Hebrew gymnasium (Herzliya)...in Tel Aviv, the town of Herzliya in the Sharon, and neighborhoods and streets in many Israeli towns and cities."[60]

The event that sparked an idea
Chaim Weizmann, a Russian Jew with an interest in science, moved as a young man to Berlin, Germany in 1892 to study biochemistry. There he became involved with some intellectual Zionists and bought into the idea of a Jewish homeland in Palestine. A few years later Weizmann moved to England to begin a career in scientific research at Manchester University. He also used his time to provide some leadership for the Zionist movement in England.

In the midst of WWI, the Allies were running out of ammunition when Weizmann came across a new way to synthesize acetone (used in the manufacture of munitions). He oversaw mass production of the chemical which allowed the Allies to win the war.

After the dissolving of the Axis Powers, namely Germany and the Ottoman Empire, at France's Versailles Palace in June 1919, one of the spoils of war for the Allies was a chunk of land in the Middle East, formerly controlled by the now-defunct Ottoman Empire. The whole area was carved up after the war and divided between France and Britain. The League of Nations recognized and enacted the 1916 Sykes-Picot Agreement which divided the Arab lands into nation-states which would be governed by outside authorities until it was deemed that the nation-states were sufficiently strong enough to rule on their own. The general areas of Lebanon and Syria were known as the French Mandate, and Iraq, Palestine, and Jordan (then called Transjordan) were given to the British, as the British Mandate.

Region of Palestine

Here it may be helpful to realize that Palestine was not a nation, such as Canada or New Zealand are nations. It was a region known as 'Palestine.' And Palestinians (such as they were known then) were no more Palestinian (as is touted by the international press today) than people who live in the north east region of the United States are known as Northeasterners. The word *Palestinian* designated a regional location where people lived not a nationality. The people who lived in this region of the Ottoman Empire were comprised of Arabs, Jews who had been living in the land and thousands of Jews who had begun to immigrate from Europe in the early and mid 1800's, and Bedouin tribes of shepherds who migrated all over the Middle East.

Back to Weizmann's Influence into Zionism

Weizmann's discovery of synthetic acetone and his sharing it opened relationship and influence with the men who ran Britain's government, so Weizmann talked with them about what he talked to everyone else about: A Jewish homeland in Palestine.

Many people in Britain were favorable to the idea, but with different motivations. Some wanted the Jews to finally have a place of their own, others were anti-Semitic in their views, wanting all the Jews out of their land and advocated putting all the Jews together somewhere (anywhere-but-here), asap.

As only God can do, He used even the worst intentions for the good of His people, because both viewpoints ended in the same result: Israel for the Jews.

The Balfour Declaration

After several years of cultivating relationship with influential men Weizmann was able to influence British policy toward a commitment to a Jewish home in Palestine. A letter from Lord Balfour to Lord Rothschild on November 2, 1917, became the first time the Zionist movement had evidence of headway toward reclaiming the Promised Land.

Foreign Office,
November 2nd, 1917

Dear Lord Rothschild,

I have much pleasure in conveying to you, on behalf of His Majesty's Government, the following declaration of sympathy with Jewish Zionist aspirations which has been submitted to, and approved by, the Cabinet.

"His Majesty's Government view with favour the establishment in Palestine of a national home for the Jewish people, and will use their best endeavours to facilitate the achievement of this object, it being clearly understood that nothing shall be done which may prejudice the civil and religious rights of existing non-Jewish communities in Palestine, or the rights and political status enjoyed by Jews in any other country."

I should be grateful if you would bring this declaration to the knowledge of the Zionist Federation.

Yours sincerely,
Arthur James Balfour [61]

So it was the wording of "nothing shall be done which may prejudice the civil and religious rights of existing non-Jewish communities in Palestine" that Weizmann went to work on next.

The next year, in 1918, Great Britain appointed Weizmann as head of the Zion Commission and sent him to Palestine to scope out the British Mandate for development. He was also tasked with establishing a peaceful relationship with the local Arabs. They assumed the local Jews would welcome the rejoining of their brothers. Because of the very poor 1918 conditions of this land, Weizmann knew that the local economy would benefit greatly from the Zionists' influx to the area. Emir Feisal was the go-to guy for the Arabs in the Ottoman Empire's former land holdings. Feisal promised to recognize Zionist claims (as designated by the British) to the land, as long as "the aims Arab nationalism were achieved in Iraq and Syria."[62] However, Feisal's support did not last long!

During these years, Weizmann was also lobbying for international recognition of the Balfour Declaration, which he accomplished in 1922 when the League of Nations officially granted the British Mandate for Palestine in which they cited a Jewish heritage and right of return.

So, it was the Allies winning WWI against Germany and the Ottoman Empire that even put Palestine on the table for the Jews to receive the land from the British.

Jerusalem before the Great War
After an early period of reconstruction by the Ottomans when the markets, mosques and some housing were refurbished, Jerusalem fell into disrepair. Between 1860 and the 1900's Jerusalem finally had a majority of her 18,000 inhabitants claiming Jewish heritage! But because of rising crime and general deterioration, many Jews moved out of the Old City walls to new garden-type neighborhoods of Jerusalem (i.e. the New City, which sprouted up outside the Old City boundary walls, heavier on the western side than the eastern side). Jewish philanthropists worldwide financially supported these moves. Sir Moses Montefiore was one such man. He was "a highly successful British merchant, (who) rebuilt the Hurvah Synagogue, established a printing press, a soup kitchen, housing for the poor, a girl's school, the city's first Jewish hospital, and the first Jewish neighborhood outside the city's walls called Mishkenot Sha'ananim (the Tranquil Abode)"[63]

Jerusalem 1917
Just as WWI was ending, Ottoman-held Jerusalem surrendered to the British Army, and General Allenby moved into the city a couple of days later at Jaffa Gate in a victory procession. This ended 400 years of Turkish rule and began 30 years of British rule. Jerusalem became the capital once again. With the British in charge, city planning was quickly underway. A new law was set in place that only "Jerusalem Stone" could be used as building materials, or minimally, as a façade. This Jerusalem

Stone provides the uniformity of color and texture found in Jerusalem today (Also, at sunset, the stone provides a pinkish-gold reflection of the setting sun that is glorious to behold. Perhaps a smallest reminder of the glory once beheld in the temple(s) there.) Over the next couple of years, social and governmental infrastructure began to form through the founding of Hebrew University, YMCA, Hadassah Hospital, the King David Hotel, the Central Post Office, and formation of more new neighborhoods outside the Old City walls. The New Jerusalem was coming to life! [64]

The Treaty of Versailles (very loosely described)
The powerful nations met at Versailles to carve up the "losers's" land after the war. The world was particularly angry with Germany for "starting it." Europe was now a shambles and worldwide 8.5 million lives had been lost and 21 million more people had been wounded. Also during 1918, a flu epidemic had hit Europe and 25 million *more* lives were lost! The Allies had lost any charity they might have held out for the Axis Powers, and managed to blame these flu deaths on the Axis Powers as well.[65] Germany had to give up land to France, Belgium, Denmark, Czechoslovakia, and Poland, reduce their military substantially, and pay reparations to the nations they destroyed. Austria-Hungary, Bulgaria, and Turkey (Ottoman Empire) also had to give up land and pay reparations.

Turkey's payment for WWI was fairly severe, probably because they beat Britain in the Battle of Gallipoli. They had to give up:

> Most of her land in Europe. Turkey was left with but a toe hold on what is considered Europe. [T]he Turkish Straits was put under the control of the League of Nations at a time when it was dominated by Britain and France. [T]he land held by Turkey in Arabia was made into a mandate - the land was ruled by the British and French until the people of the areas were ready to govern themselves. Syria and Lebanon went to France while Iraq, Transjordan and Palestine went to Britain.
>
> Armies from Britain, France, Greece and Italy occupied what was left of Turkey - the area known as Asia Minor."[65]

The part we are most interested in is the area which is now Israel and Jordan (formerly Palestine and Transjordan).

The British requested this particular section of land over any other particular land (i.e. the Lebanon section) in order to create a homeland for the Jewish people, which the men we discussed earlier had been requesting from the British leadership. "The Mandate was international recognition for the stated purpose of 'establishing in Palestine a national home for the Jewish people.'"[66]

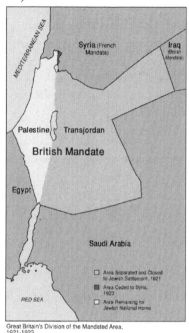

Great Britain's Division of the Mandated Area, 1921-1923

The fact that the British mandate included references to the Balfour Declaration and the establishment of a Jewish homeland was a severe blow to the Arabs. Partly to try and mollify this disappointment, the British split the Palestine mandate into two distinct areas, using the Jordan River as a natural boundary. The British claimed that Jewish immigration would be confined to the West of the river. The East of the river, which represented three quarters of the whole mandate area was to be reserved for the Arabs alone.[67]

Two-State Solution
Because the Arabs were mad, the British divided the land they had promised to the Jews to try to satisfy the Arabs. So of the original ~45,000 square miles of land mass, 77% went to the Arabs and 16.8 % went to the Jews. The remaining tidbits of the Gaza Strip, Golan Heights, and West Bank were divvied up with Syria, Egypt and Jordan. Of the 16.8 % of the land that was given to the Jews, only 6.7% was habitable land. Ten per cent of the entire British Mandate was the Negev Desert/Wilderness, all unusable, uninhabitable land. All of it went to the Jews. Major disadvantage!

This Arab-Jewish two-state solution occurred in 1922 and is known as the Churchill White Paper (though Sir Herbert Samuel was a large influencer). It gave the name "Transjordan" to the East portion of the British Mandate and gave it to Emir Abdullah to rule. This White Paper suggested limitations on immigration to what the Palestinian economy could support and suggested establishing self-government in Palestine by the Jews.[68] However Jews were FORBIDDEN to immigrate to or own land in Transjordan!

1920-1948

Between 1860 and 1948 the population growth in Jerusalem was nearly 1,000%. They went from 18,000 to 160,000 souls, 100,000 of whom were Jews.[63] (Running these numbers shows that there are plenty of non-Jews immigrating to the Land at this time too, but we will get to that another time!) *Unrest* describes the Land during this time. The British were phasing themselves out, but there was a prevailing two-fold question. What would the future of Palestine look like and how would that effect what Jerusalem looked like. The rising tensions between Jews and Arabs brought on horrible riots in 1920 and 1929. Then the Arabs revolted from 1936-1939. Suddenly this land that nobody really wanted, everyone wanted, and they wanted it exclusively! The British Army quelled many riots. [69]

Due to some odd laws enforced by the British and set in place to try to stifle the Arab raids, riots, revolts etc., the Arabs were provided guns by the British, but the Jews were not allowed to have them. It makes no natural sense because the British were supposed to be helping the Jews set in place a peaceable self-sustaining government, ruled by Jews. But I think God already had in mind a plan that would "shock and awe" His people into realizing that He was the One calling them home to this Land, and He would be their Protector. This no-guns-for-Jews law was enforced (punishable by imprisonment or death) even up to the day Israel became a sovereign nation. The Jews had to smuggle guns and ammunition into their borders. Jewish immigration was severely limited too, even though by designation this land had been set aside for the Jews of the world to come "home." From the time of the White Papers of 1939 and for the next five years during World War II, when Jews needed a safe home the most, only 75,000 Jews were allowed into the Palestine Region. So people were smuggled in as well. This unjust decision and its enforcement contributed to the deaths of 6,000,000 Jewish people in camps all over Europe. Many European Jews would not have chosen to come to the forming Jewish state even if the borders had been wide open to them. But during this time Arab immigration to the Palestine Region was unenforced. They poured in from neighboring nations because of the superior economic conditions created by the Zionists (just like Weizmann had said).[70]

This illegal Arab immigration was allowed to flow unchecked, when the Jewish immigration laws were enforced, probably because Britain was more sensitive to the Arabs' claims during a war-time because they needed to maintain peaceful control of the Suez Canal.

Interestingly, there are many accounts of Jews and Arabs growing up together, peacefully co-existing for over 700 years, even being friends, in Jerusalem and other Palestinian towns around the British Mandate land. It was the rise of one brutal Arab, who had aspirations to rule a pan-Arabic empire in the Middle East, which began the Arab-Israeli conflict as we know it in the 20th and 21st centuries.

Start of the Modern Arab-Israeli Conflict

In 1920, Haj Amin Muhammad al Husseini (yes, he is a relative of the family Hussein you are familiar with) was the grand mufti of Jerusalem. He was the Imam of the Al Aqsa mosque, which was the highest Muslim authority in the British Mandate. Al Aqsa is the gray domed mosque located on the temple mount in Jerusalem (former location of Solomon's Temple). Al Husseini used anti-Jewish propaganda to drive as many wedges between the Jewish and Arab communities as he could. He eliminated, or rather murdered, Jews and Arab who he considered a threat to his control.[71]

Unfortunately his propaganda worked again and again. The Arabs and the Jews separated themselves more and more, with riots erupting more often as time progressed toward Israel becoming the homeland of the Jews as recognized by the United Nations.

November 29, 1947—UN General Assembly, Resolution 181

In late fall of 1947, two years after the world had been through a second catastrophic global clash, world leaders meet at the newly formed (1945) United Nations to vote on resolution 181, which called for the partition of the British Mandate to be divided into (another) two states. One for the Arabs and one for the Jews. The following is a map[72] of the proposal and a record of UN member countries' vote.

Partition Plan 1947 (UN Resolution 181)

United Nations General Assembly Resolution 181 called for the partition of the British-ruled Palestine Mandate into a Jewish state and an Arab state. It was approved on November 29, 1947 with 33 votes in favor, 13 against, 10 abstentions and one absent...

The resolution was accepted by the Jews in Palestine, yet rejected by the Arabs in Palestine and the Arab states.

Here is the tally for the vote **For: 33** Australia, Belgium, Bolivia, Brazil, Byelorussian S.S.R., Canada, Costa Rica, Czechoslovakia, Denmark, Dominican Republic, Ecuador, France, Guatemala, Haiti, Iceland, Liberia, Luxemburg, Netherlands, New Zealand, Nicaragua, Norway, Panama, Paraguay, Peru, Philippines, Poland, Sweden, Ukrainian S.S.R., Union of South Africa, U.S.A., U.S.S.R., Uruguay, Venezuela.

Against: 13 Afghanistan, Cuba, Egypt, Greece, India, Iran, Iraq, Lebanon, Pakistan, Saudi Arabia, Syria, Turkey, Yemen.

Abstained: 10 Argentina, Chile, China, Colombia, El Salvador, Ethiopia, Honduras, Mexico, United Kingdom, Yugoslavia.

The Odds were Against Them

As the British rule drew to a close, the five Arab nations that surrounded Israel began to band together with the common goal of tightening a noose around the neck of the new State of Israel even as she was in the weak and vulnerable time of being birthed. Egypt, Transjordan, Syria, Lebanon, and Iraq threw everything they had into seeing her destroyed.

May 14-15, 1948 in Israel
A new nation was born. It was so declared by David ben Gurion.

> At midnight on May 14, 1948, the Provisional Government of Israel proclaimed the new State of Israel. On that same date the United States, in the person of President Truman, recognized the provisional Jewish government as de facto authority of the new Jewish state (de jure recognition was extended on January 31). The U.S. delegates to the U.N. and top ranking State Department officials were angered that Truman released his recognition statement to the press without notifying them first. On May 15, 1948, the Arab states issued their response statement and Arab armies invaded Israel and the first Arab-Israeli war began.[73]

I find it interesting that the proclaiming of Israel's statehood occurred after sundown on a Friday, which made it a Shabbat in Israel. How appropriate after 1800 years of work, work, work to become a nation again, that their first day would fall on a holy day of rest. However rest would have to wait. Eleven minutes after her re-birth, the US recognized Israel publically. While the Jews danced in the streets, the Arab tanks crossed the newly declared borders in defiance of Israel's sovereignty. War loomed for this fledgling nation.

Elsewhere in Europe: The Holocaust
While all this "becoming a nation" was happening in the Palestine Region, Jews were being systematically hunted down and murdered by God's enemy (though the Nazi Party of Germany). Because the horrors of the Holocaust could (and DO) fill many volumes that are written much better than I can, I will only give the briefest of descriptions.

It has seemed to me that the Holocaust occurred because of a frog-in-hot-water kind of mentality of the Jews of the day. Though I can hardly fault them for not resisting. For generation upon generation the Jews of Europe were considered underclass citizens—if even allowed citizenship. Though they ran the banks, jewelry stores, and department stores, and earned the Nobel prizes in science, math, and the arts in way-disproportionate numbers, the Jews were ridiculed, parodied,

114

discriminated against and singled out for harassment. And after a while, it always let up.

But not this time.

In fall 1939, the German discrimination turned to actual murder. Then mass murders! July 2, 1940, Herman Goring (the SS's #2 man) assigned Reinhard Heydrich the task of finding a "final solution for the Jewish question of Europe." They decided to kill them all, men, women, and children. "In early December, the first extermination camp, Chelmno, went into operation. There Jews began to be murdered with carbon monoxide gas generated by large diesel engines that pumped gas into gas chambers"[74]

Many, many Jewish families report similar mindsets early on: "Sure it was getting bad in the next country, or the next county or town over, but it wouldn't come here. Things would work themselves out if we just keep our heads down. It will all blow over. Things will get better." But it didn't. Thousands after thousands of Jews were rousted from their business, their commutes, their beds and hoisted into the backs of military convoy trucks.

They were counted and checked off of lists and herded into overcrowded cattle cars. The trains snaked though rural communities adding always to their burgeoning cargo of Jews. Finally the trains vomited them out in the death camps such as Auschwitz under a sign spouting "Work makes you free."

But the back-breaking and spirit-breaking work here, only offered freedom in death.

Yad Vashem is a memorial and museum in the outskirts of the new city of Jerusalem that has gathered, and is still gathering the names of the millions of Jews who were murdered. The following chart[74] from *Yad Vashem*'s website offers a country by country break down of the people.

Country	Pre-war Jewish Population	Minimum Loss	Maximum Loss
Austria	185,000	50,000	50,000
Belgium	65,700	28,900	28,900
Bohemia and Moravia	118,310	78,150	78,150
Bulgaria	50,000	0	0
Denmark	7,800	60	60
Estonia	4,500	1,500	2,000
Finland	2,000	7	7
France	350,000	77,320	77,320
Germany	566,000	134,500	141,500
Greece	77,380	60,000	67,000
Hungary	825,000	550,000	569,000
Italy	44,500	7,680	7,680
Latvia	91,500	70,000	71,500
Lithuania	168,000	140,000	143,000
Luxembourg	3,500	1,950	1,950
Netherlands	140,000	100,000	100,000

Norway	1,700	762	762
Poland	3,300,000	2,900,000	3,000,000
Romania	609,000	271,000	287,000
Slovakia	88,950	68,000	71,000
Soviet Union	3,020,000	1,000,000	1,100,000
Yugoslavia	78,000	56,200	63,300
Total	9,796,840	5,596,029	5,860,129
Rounded	9.8 million	5.6 Million	5.8 million

It is a little overwhelming to see such high numbers and realize that entire extended families were sometimes wiped out and family lines lost forever. However, it is far more disconcerting that EVERY single family now living in the ENTIRE country of Israel has lost a member or many members to the Holocaust.

The few Holocaust survivors remaining in Israel are quickly dying out. Many live below the poverty line, but all are respected. I've witnessed on a Tel Aviv city bus a punk kid with attitude get out of his seat to help a couple of survivors get their grocery cart up the bus stairs and then give them his seat. The punk kid stood instead. The survivors living in Israel are honored as if they are the grandmother or great grandfather of everyone in the nation. There is a special holiday in the spring when a siren wails out a mournful sound for two minutes, and the entire country stops, people shopping in the squares, taxis and buses and cars on the street. All movement halts as those who were killed are honored in our memories. May this bit of human history never find its way to our history books again.

*End note concerning the land conditions in Israel. The stripping of the trees to avoid taxes led to erosion; it disrupted natural cycles of evaporation and carbon dioxide/oxygen exchange bringing about desert conditions or swamps to overtake the land. One of the first things the Jews coming home did was to begin to plant trees. They also worked on the land to cultivate crops, and drain the swamps, rid the land of disease carrying mosquitoes. They planted forests of trees. Even today, there are forests where individuals around the world can buy a tree to plant in Israel. But when you visit, or see pictures, remember EVERY tree in Israel has been planted.

When one realizes the care and time that goes into planting individual trees, the weight of devastation of the fire on Mount Carmel during Hanukkah 2010 is much more apparent. Five million trees went up in smoke, and will have to be replanted.[75]

CHAPTER 9

ISHMAEL THESE 2,500 YEARS

Topics: Word definitions, tribal ancestry, Muhammad's family curse, Islam's beginnings, problems within the Qu'ran.

Let's start with a few dictionary.com definitions to make sure we correctly use words that we may have once thought interchangeable:

Jew: noun—One of a scattered group of people that traces it descent from the Biblical Hebrews or from postexilic adherents of Judaism. An Israelite. A person whose religion is Judaism. A subject of the ancient kingdom of Judah.
Jewish: the adjective use of Jew
Judaism: noun—the monotheistic religion of the Jews
Jewry: noun—Jews collectively
Semitic: Adjective form of Semite
Semite: Noun—any person descended from Noah's son Shem. Includes the Akkadians, Canaanites, Phoenicians, Hebrews, and Arabs
Arab: noun—A member of a Semitic people inhabiting Arabia and other countries of the Middle East; a member of any Arabic-speaking people.
Arabic vs. Arabian: the adjective form of Arab is interchangeable, but generally "Arabian" designates from the Arabian Peninsula.
Islam: noun—**A:** the religious faith of Muslims, based on the words and religious system founded by the prophet Muhammad and taught by the Koran, the basic principle of which is absolute submission to a unique and personal god, Allah.
Islam B: the whole body of Muslim believers, their civilization, and the countries in which theirs is the dominant religion.
Islamic: Adjective used to refer to the religion of Islam
Muslim: Noun—adherent of Islam, Adjective—of or pertaining to the religion, law, or civilization of Islam.
Moslem: a variant spelling of Muslim, literally: "one who submits"
Christian: Noun or adjective—a believer in Jesus as the promised Messiah of Judaism

Messianic: Adjective—literally "of or relating to the Messiah." But is also a common term for Jews who have accepted Jesus as the promised savior of Judaism. Considered derogatory in Israel.

So you can have a Semite who is either Jewish or Arabic. You can have an Arab who is Jewish, Muslim or Christian, or have a Jew who is Jewish or Muslim (though a Jew who has converted to Islam would be certainly rare!) You cannot have a Muslim who is a Christian. He would be an Arab Christian since Muslim designates the religion and Arab the heritage. A Jew by blood or by religion who believes that Jesus is the promised Messiah is not considered to be "converted to Christianity" and therefore a Christian, except by his own peers/religion; he would be called "Messianic." In Israel and other Jewish circles, Messianic Jews are hated and considered dead by their religious family members because they have given up the Jewish religion. However in Christian circles, "Messianic believers" are generally highly revered.

I ran into a slight snag as I tried to relate the descendants of Abraham's son Ishmael to Biblical tribes mentioned and then equate them to their modern Arabic Tribes. As you can see below of the different family trees and charts as related to the Biblical names, even at the first generation, the names do not match. The family tree below is taken from an Islamic website.[76]

Family Tree of Prophet Muhammad

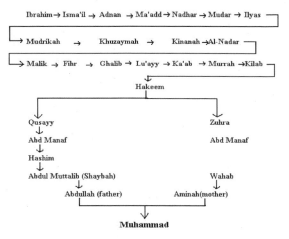

120

This covers from Abraham in the 17th century BC 24 generations to Muhammad (who is the founder of Islam in 610 AD) born in 570 AD. The descendants of Ishmael scattered across the Middle East and northern Africa.[77] The peoples listed in the Bible as being descended from Ishmael are (of course) the Ishmaelites, from Genesis 25:13-18:

> These are the names of the sons of Ishmael, listed in the order of their birth: Nebaioth the firstborn of Ishmael, Kedar, Adbeel, Mibsam, Mishma, Dumah, Massa, Hadad, Tema, Jetur, Naphish and Kedemah. These were the sons of Ishmael, and these are the names of the twelve tribal rulers according to their settlements and camps. Altogether, Ishmael lived a hundred and thirty-seven years. He breathed his last and died, and he was gathered to his people. His descendants settled in the area from Havilah to Shur, near the border of Egypt, as you go toward Asshur. And they lived in hostility toward all their brothers.

The following chart[78] is borrowed from Dan Gibson who has made it his life's work to trace the modern Arabic tribes' ancestry. Visit his site at nabataea.net.

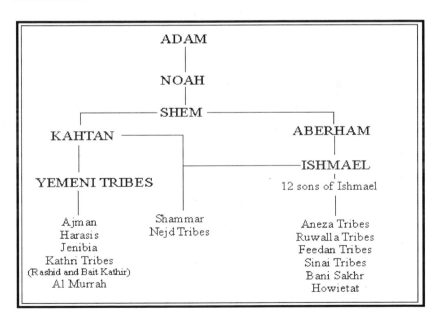

"The Biblical record of Ishmael gives us the names of the 12 sons, but no clue as to how they might be connected to the modern Bedouin Tribes."[78]

For all you chart lovers and studiers, here is the best "Founding of the Nations" chart I have come across. http://nabataea.net/foundingnations.html.

Moving forward, here is how Muhammad founded Islam:

Muhammad was born in 570 AD in Mecca (located on the west side of the Arabian Peninsula). His parents were both dead by the time he was six, and he never learned to read.

> The young orphan was then raised primarily by his uncle, for whom he worked as a shepherd. At age 9 (some sources say 12), he joined his uncle on a caravan to Syria. As a young man, Muhammad worked as a camel driver between Syria and Arabia. Soon he established a career managing caravans on behalf of merchants. Through his travel first with his uncle and later in his career, Muhammad came into contact with people of many nationalities and faiths, including Jews, Christians and pagans. At age 25, Muhammad was employed by Khadija, a wealthy Meccan widow 15 years his senior. The two were married, and by all accounts enjoyed a loving and happy marriage. Early records report that "God comforted him through her, for she made his burden light." Although polygamy was common practice at the time, Muhammad took no other wife than Khadija until her death 24 years later.[79]

Incidentally, Khadija was Jewish.[80]

However, it is interesting to note that Muhammad's life story begins, like everyone's does, before he was born. I came across some family background information in Dr. Gene Little's book, *The Mystery of Islam,*[80] that in light of generational curses and blessings as described in Genesis, offers some little-known insights into Muhammad's struggles on the spirit level.

It started with Muhammad's grandfather, Abu Muttalib ibn Hashim (ibn just designates "son of" the same way "ben" does in Hebrew). Abu Muttalib was apparently the "keeper" of the sacred stone *Ka'ba* in Mecca. (We will see this stone come into importance in Islam shortly.) Apparently he also rediscovered an ancient well called *Zamzam*, which had been filled in during a tribal dispute. He made it usable again. Water is an important commodity in the desert climate of the Middle East. So "for this good deed, Abu Muttalib was given lucrative rights to distribute its life-giving waters."[81]

The item of interest comes in when Abu Muttalib prayed to the god of the *Ka'ba* to grant him 10 sons (he only had 1 at the time), and in return, Abu would sacrifice one of his sons to this god of the *Ka'ba*. Well, it happened. Abu Muttalib got his ten sons. But when the time to sacrifice came, the youngest one Abn Allah was chosen, and it didn't go over so well with the family. Abu Muttalib consulted a witch to inquire whether the god of the *Ka'ba* would accept a substitute and what that might be. Through divination, they arrived at the idea that 100 camels would be the substitute price.

The camels were sacrificed and life seemed to go along just fine for the youngest son, Abn Allah. But the principle of sewing and reaping had already been enacted. And the consequence of sin is death.

Abn Allah died just before his son (Abu Mattalib's grandson) was born. Kutam was the son's given name, Muhammad was the name he later went by. Muhammad's care reverted first to a Bedouin mother named Halima for nursing. Muhammad's mother, Amina, then died when Muhammad was six. Muhammad then reverted back to his grandfather, Abu Muttalib. Two years later, Abu Muttalib was dead too. Muhammad then lived under the care of his uncle Abu Talib. Later Abu Talib became the head of the Hashimite clan. (Remember the name "Hashimite" from the country of Jordan's full name? The Hashimite Kingdom of Jordan? Same family.)

Then, Muhammad's sons all died in infancy except one, Ibrahim, who was born to Muhammad's slave Mary the Copt. Ibrahim died as a toddler. That is a lot of death in one little branch of this family, especially when all the deaths attributed to the one "survivor's" new religion are factored in. Perhaps it was only the witch's idea that the camels would suffice as a sacrifice substitute, because it seems like death moved in to claim this whole part of Abu Muttalib's family from his ill-conceived "deal."

It was in 610 that Muhammad received his first visitation/vision from whom he referred to after-the-fact as "the angel Gabriel"

> Muhammad reported that while in a trance-like state, the Angel Gabriel appeared to him and said "Proclaim!" But like Moses, Muhammed was a reluctant prophet. He replied, "I am not a proclaimer." The angel persisted, and the Prophet repeatedly resisted, until the angel finally overwhelmed Muhammad and commanded him:
>
> *Proclaim in the name of your Lord who created!*
> *Created man from a clot of blood.*
> *Proclaim: Your Lord is the Most Generous,*
> *Who teaches by the pen;*
> *Teaches man what he knew not.* (Qur'an 96:1-3)[79]

After several more visits, Muhammad gained enough confidence to begin spreading the words this angel had revealed to him. Over the course of three years, he gained 40 followers. "Muhammad's message to his countrymen was to convert from pagan polytheism, immorality and materialism, repent from evil and worship Allah, the only true God."[79] His message was not well-received and Muhammad and his 40 followers were made fun of and had rocks and dirt thrown on them as they prayed.

> Persecution continued to increase until Muhammad received some welcome news: he had gained followers in the city of Yathrib, 280 miles north of Mecca. The city was in need of a strong leader, and a delegation from Yathrib proposed that Muhammad take the job. In return, they pledged to worship Allah only, obey Muhammad and defend him and his followers to the death. Allah revealed to Muhammed his approval of this arrangement, and Muhammad made plans to escape to Yathrib.

The leaders in Mecca heard of the planned escape, and attempted to prevent it. But Muhammad and his close friend Abu Bakr managed to make a narrow escape north out of the city, evading a Meccan search party and arriving safely in Yathrib. This event is celebrated by Muslims as the *Hijira.* The year in which it occurred, 622, is the date at which the Muslim calendar begins. Yathrib was renamed Medinat al-Nabi, "the City of the Prophet," and is now known simply as Medina, "the City."[79]

In Islam's infancy, Muhammad, in trying to gain the Jews as converts, "borrowed" several tenants of the Jewish faith. He encouraged followers to pray toward Jerusalem, he set up a kosher diet, and he declared Saturday as the holy day. However,

Once it was clear the Jews would not accept him, Muhammad began to minimize or eliminate the Jewish influence on his beliefs. For example, he shifted the direction of prayers from Jerusalem to Mecca, made Friday his special day of prayer, and renounced the Jewish dietary laws (except for the prohibition on eating pork). Originally, he said the Arabs were descendants of Abraham through his son Ishmael, but in the Koran Abraham's connection to the Jews is denied, with Muhammad asserting that Abraham is only the patriarch of Islam, not Judaism as well, because he "surrendered himself to Allah."[82]

In addition to the changing of his religion's tenets, Muhammad was so angry at the Jews because they would not come on board with his new religion that he used his power to expel two Jewish tribes from Medina, and in a third tribe he massacred all the men and sold into slavery all the women and children. He also then included a number of "inflammatory statements" in his tenets, (i.e. the Qu'ran) against the Jews. This of course lent suggestion and "rightness" to the ill-treatment of Jews throughout the centuries, even currently. Muhammad's "neighboring tribes were overpowered, and forced to submit to Allah or the sword. A total of 76 campaigns were fought. His own tribe threatened to crush him and his religion."[83]

> In 630, Muhammad and his forces marched to Mecca and defeated it. The Prophet rededicated the Ka'ba temple to Allah, witnessed the conversion to Islam of nearly the entire Meccan population, then returned to Medina. Muhammad died in 632, having conquered nearly all of Arabia for Islam.
>
> By 634, Islam had taken over the entire Arabian Peninsula. Within 100 years of Muhammad's death, it had reached the Atlantic in one direction and borders of China in the other. This success was due in large part to the military and political abilities of Muhammad's successors, the caliphs.[79]

I have to wonder about these conversions to Islam because of the deep violence with which actual followers of Islam resort to...Armies? Battles? Killings? How many people of this era of polytheistic worship are not going to say they accept Allah's purposes under threat of death? I mean, what is one more "god?"

The Changing Story of Islam

Muhammad made changes to his religion as he was forming it, whether of his own design or a more diabolical origin (such as Satan appearing to Muhammad as an angel who called himself "Gabriel"). If something didn't fit properly, or if something needed changes for political purposes, (or if it just didn't fit Muhammad's lifestyle) Muhammed amended his Qu'ran. And the most recent "statement" was the one his followers were supposed to obey because it superseded all previous writings. This is called *abrogation* and the tenet can be found in S 2:106: (S=surrah, the standard division of the passages similar to the Bible's books or chapters.)

> *"Such of our Revelation as we abrogate or cause to be forgotten, we bring in place one better or the like*

126

thereof. Knoweth not that Allah is Able to do all things?"

And in S 3:85:

And when we put a revelation in place of another revelation and Allah knoweth best what he revealeth. They say Lo; Thou art but interventing. Most of them know not!

So after a more modern revelation becomes "scripture" this second passage basically says if someone says "you're just making that up for convenience sake," then the Muslim can say "you don't know what you are talking about." Sounds self-serving and slippery to me.

Tidbits from early in the Qu'ran:

S:2:47: *"Children of Israel to remember the favor I bestowed upon you and how I exalted you above all nations."*

Allah declares to the Israelites S:17:103: *"Dwell in the Land. When the promise of the hearafter comes to be fulfilled, we shall assemble you all together."*

Apparently, these are verses in the Qu'ran that Muslims are allowed to "forget." God does not revoke His promise to the Children of Israel that they would live in the borders of Israel that God Himself set up. Even based on their own holy revelations, Muslims should not be disputing it. It is written that the land of Israel belongs to those we now call the Jews.

One of the most famous slippery set of Qu'ranic scriptures occurs with a Quraysh tribe. Muhammad wanted them to join his religion, but they were firmly against worshipping any gods besides the three pagan goddesses they already worshipped, *Al Lat, Al'Uzza* and *Al Manat,* and they felt threatened by Muhammad's prodding. Since the Quraysh tribe was getting feisty about all his pushing, to calm things down and appease the Quraysh people, Muhammad went to worship Allah at the rock Ka'ba and mentioned in his prayers (aloud, of course, so they would hear) how impressive he found this tribe and their goddesses, that their prayers to these three beautiful goddesses was good. Little expresses it this way, as Muhammad was worshipping at the rock *Ka'ba,* he "praised them and approved of their intercession saying: Did you consider *Al Lat* and *Al'Uzza* and *Al Manat, the third, the other? Those cranes exalted* (female goddesses) *between heaven and earth like angels. Their intercession is expected. Their likes are not neglected.*"[84]

In other words, Muhammad expressed his own "divine approval" for worshipping gods besides Allah. While this went over very well with the Quraysh tribe who decided that Islam was no longer a threat, it did not go over so well with Muhammad's "angel Gabriel." Muhammad was told by "Gabriel" that Satan had entered his mind and given him those verses. But it was ok, because most other godly prophets had failed too, and Allah would give him new and improved verses to take their place.

So Muhammad named those verses *"the Satanic Verses"* and announced his newest revelation: (S. 53: 19-23)

> Have you (thought) upon *Al Lat* and *Al'Uzza* and *Al Manat, the other third goddess? Have you male children and Allah female? This is indeed an unfair division! They are no other than empty named goddesses. Allah has not revealed concerning them anything to authorize their worship.*

According to Little, "The whole 'mistake' was quickly 'erased' out of the Koran, but the story was remembered by Ibn Sa'd, and is recorded in his Hadith."[84]

According to the Hadith (the sacred Islamic writings), during Muhammad's final sickness he "repeatedly asked Allah to *'curse the Jews and Christians because they took the graves of their prophets as places of worship' Sahih al-Bukhari,* Vol 7 #706. Interestingly enough, pilgrimages are now made by Muslims to Muhammad's grave and prayers are offered there for his intercession!"[85] I find it laughable that despite Muhammad's judgment of Jews and Christians, most Muslim pilgrims base their visits to his grave on Muhammad's own words "Who goes to *Hajj* and does not visit me has insulted me!" which asks for the same honor that he asked Allah to curse. I am so glad that as Christians we do have an Intercessor to pray to, and whose grave is empty!

When Muhammad received a "new revelation" that it was acceptable to force his adopted son to divorce his wife so that Muhammad could marry her, it was scandalous, even for the prophet. Here was his convenient, (and might I add "really specific") new revelation: S. 33:37-38

> *And when Zayd divorced his wife, we gave her to you in marriage, so that it should become legitimate for true believers to wed the wives of their adopted sons if they divorce them. God's will must needs be done. No blame shall be attached to the Prophet for doing what is sanctioned for him by God.*

I think one of Muhammad's 14 wives, A'isha, hit it squarely on the head when she said of this "new revelation," "Truly thy Lord makes haste to do thy bidding." I can almost hear the sarcasm dripping!

More Problems within the Text of the Qu'ran.

Gene Little's description of the Qu'ran being a "bipolar book" is right on in my opinion. **Killing and showing mercy are cancelled out in this same verse** of the Qu'ran:

> *When the sacred months have passed, slay the idolaters wherever you find them, and take them prisoner, and besiege them, and prepare for them each ambush. But if they repent and establish worship and pay the legal tax, then leave their way free. Lo! Allah is Forgiving, Merciful* (S.9:5).

Muhammad changed the **direction for prayer** from a choice to face east or west, to a command first to face Jerusalem and then to face only Mecca. (2:115, 2:142, 2:144) and the verses are so close together it must make the adherent's head's spin!

Surrah 5:90 forbids consumption of **wine**, yet 16:11 implies it is fine, and to top it off, heaven is described in 47:15 as having rivers of wine. Surrah 26:191-196 talks about how this "holy revelation" is given in pure **Arabic language**, yet scholars have found words from Egyptian, Assyrian, Coptic, Persian, Syrian, Greek, and (wait for it...) Hebrew languages throughout the Qu'ran.[86] Even the **account of creation** is confused in Islam. Muhammad states it happens in two days in Surrah 41:9-12, but Surrahs 7:54 and 10:4 both relate to a six-day creation.

Personally, my biggest problem with the Qu'ran [you know, setting aside that whole "kill the infidel (umm...me!)" bit] is the leeway to lie. The Qu'ran states that lying is okay, as long as it was not purposeful. However, there are three instances when, according to the Hadith, Muslims are free to lie intentionally.

1. In holy war (jihad).
2. To bring reconciliation among hostile Muslims.
3. Between a husband and wife to bring reconciliation.

Westerners who try to conduct "peace talks" with the Muslim world should be aware of this, and realize that since Islam has declared Jihad on the West, they can lie (with religious applause) for any reason. Therefore their words can never be trusted. Whether it be the big lie (i.e. the holocaust never happened; we just want to live peacefully with the Israelis on our land of Palestine; the Jews used to have good lives when they lived among us for centuries, we invite them back) or the little lies (we will stop the rockets if they stop killing our children).

How different Islam is to Christianity, where truth is paramount, where the One we are to immolate calls Himself "the Truth!" Telling the truth is one of our 10 basic tenets (which we received from Judaism). But we should not rejoice that our religion wins again for being the better. As Christians we are commanded to love our "enemies," do good to those who despitefully use us. We should pray for the Muslims that the Truthteller will visit them. People of the Muslim faith have been duped by The Big Lie designed by the enemy of the human race to separate them from God. God desires that NONE should perish. Jesus came to set the captives free; and Muslims are bound by the lies they have believed for centuries. They are not the enemy anyway, the one who has bound them is the enemy.

Jesus is appearing in dreams and visions to Muslims in unprecedented numbers. They are accepting Him as their savior, forsaking Islam forever!

CHAPTER 10

LESSON: PALESTINIAN PROBLEM

Topics: How the "Palestinian Problem" got to where it is today. Ruling Bodies of Judea, maps, "Aliyah," population exchange, birth of the nations of the Middle East, the Big Lie.

First off, even the word "Palestinian" is a problem. The name was made up by the Romans to describe the region (not a nation) when they conquered Israel in 73 AD. Romans squashed the final rebellion in 133 AD, renamed the area and the name stuck.[87] Remember the Philistines? Those hated enemies of Israel that they had a problem conquering over the centuries? As an added insult to the miniscule population left alive in Israel, the Romans renamed their land "Philistia" which turned into "Palaestina." According to Moshe Sharon, *Palaestina* commonly referred

> to the coastal region, and shortly thereafter, the whole of the area inland to the west of the Jordan River. The latter extension occurred when the Roman authorities, following the suppression of the Bar Kokhba rebellion in the 2nd century CE, renamed "Provincia Judea" (Iudaea Province; originally derived from the name "Judah") to "Syria Palaestina", in order to complete the dissociation with Judaea.[89]

So the name "Palestinian" actually refers to the few **Jews** who were left after Israel was demolished by the Romans.

Over the centuries this land was invaded and conquered many times. The following is a list of the ruling bodies and their years of "service:"

- Hebrew Bible/Old Testament period—self rule
- Persian rule (538 BC) Classical antiquity
- Hellenistic rule (333 BC)
- Hasmonean dynasty (140 BC)
- Roman rule (63 BC)
- Byzantine (Eastern Roman) rule (330–640 AD)

- Arab Caliphate rule (638–1099 AD)

  - Umayyad rule (661–750 AD)
  - Abbasid rule (750–969 AD)
  - Fatimid rule (969–1099 AD)

- Crusader rule (1099–1187 AD)
- Mamluk rule (1270–1516 AD)
- Ottoman rule (1516–1831 AD)
- Egyptian rule (1831–1841)
- Ottoman rule (1841–1917)
- British Mandate (1920–1948)
- UN partition and the 1948 War of Independence

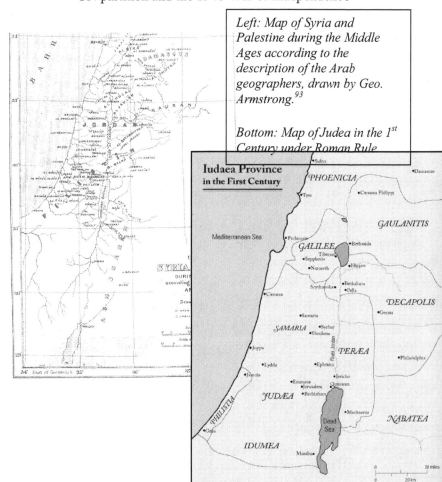

Left: Map of Syria and Palestine during the Middle Ages according to the description of the Arab geographers, drawn by Geo. Armstrong.[93]

Bottom: Map of Judea in the 1st Century under Roman Rule.

Zionists from Europe and Yemen began immigrating home to the Promised Land at the end of the 19th century. Their return is called "Aliyah" which means "to go up" in Hebrew, a language that, even while the immigrants were arriving, was being revived. This First Aliyah between 1881 and 1903 brought 25-35,000 Jews to the Land. These brave men and women who had been bankers, lawyers and professionals in their former lives established new settlements on the barren, treeless, and in some places, swampy land. They established the current cities of *Rishon LeZion, Rosh Pina, Zikhron Ya'aqov,* and *Gedera.*[89] They farmed the land.

Between 1904 and 1914 about 40,000 Jews from Russia and Poland made up the Second Aliyah. For the most part, they were idealistic people inspired by commune-style living, as presented by the Russian Empire. They founded Kibbutzim (plural of Kibbutz) all over Israel to raise crops in agriculture settlements. The original Kibbutz was Degania, founded in 1909.

So immigration by Jews (and incidentally others too) was pretty hopping until World War II when the British enforced unrealistic controls on Jewish immigration, but not on other ethnicities.

So, skip forward about 35 years to 1948. Israel becomes a nation, and the Jews of the world are supposed to come and live there. But there is a question of what to do with the non-Jews who lived there. The wars will be covered in another chapter, but there was some massive fighting that swept through the Holy Land. The following statistics and information is compiled and summarized from Joan Peters' work in *From Time Immemorial.*[90] It is a well-documented, primary-source research tool that she complied over several years and published in 1984. When Ms Peters began the work she was Pro-Palestinian; when she heard the whole story, she leaned more toward the Jews' plight.

In 1948, there were more than 850,000 Jews living in Arab-lead nations. In 1984, there were fewer than 29,000. What happened to them?

Yemen—50,000 Jews came to Israel from Yemen via "Operation Magic Carpet" under great duress.

Iraq—123,000 Jews came to Israel from Iraq in just the years between 1949 and 1952. These Jews had prospered in this area formerly called Babylon from 1200 years <u>before</u> the Muslim conquest in 634 AD (P. 43).

Egypt—75,000 Jews lived in a community dating back to before the Babylonian Captivity. In 3 months, (August to November of 1949) 20,000 of them fled to Israel. In "1956 thousands were interned without trial, while still other thousands were served with deportation papers and ordered to leave within a few days; their property was confiscated, their assets frozen" (p.49). Then those who had been imprisoned, were led in chains to boats and forced "to sign statements that they left voluntarily" with no possessions.

Morocco—From northern Africa more than 300,000 Jews fled to Israel, 250,000 from Morocco alone. These families had lived in this region since 586 BC, nearly always under persecution after Islam was born.

Algeria—Jews settled in what is now called Algeria (then North Africa) with the "first settlers, the Phoenicians" and left 2,500 years later. The Jewish population was around 140,000 in 1948, and it practically disappeared within months. Thousands to moved Israel, and 125,000 went to France, who had recently overthrown the government in Algeria.

Tunisia—Jews lived continuously in Tunisia for about 2,300 years, and of the 105,000 Jews in Tunisia in 1948, 50,000 immigrated to Israel, and roughly 50,000 to France and elsewhere.

Syria—Jews lived here from Biblical times. Around 1917 there were about 35,000 Syrian Jews. In 1943, 30,000 still remained, because life was relatively normal compared to the surrounding nations where Jews were being slaughtered. But in 1961, when Muslims took control, Jews were prohibited from leaving, and they publically announced that all refugees caught would be put to death! By early 1947, only 13,000 remained. Most left covertly through secret routes, and even the *New York Herald Tribune* reported that Syria had launched an investigation into the disappearance of some 17,000 Syrian Jews.

Lebanon—Here lived a small Jewish community of 55 families in 1862. They were descents of those who left Israel during the Roman Invasion and from those Spanish Jews who escaped the Inquisition of 1492. By 1958, Lebanon was the only Arab country where the Jews had increased in number (to 9,000), probably due to the Christian-dominated government. When the Arabs took over during the "Muslim Revolt" the Jews began to flee in great numbers.

Libya—Jews immigrated to Libya before the destruction of Jerusalem by the Romans in 70 AD and were most often used to settle land as a buffer between Libya and enemies of Lybia. During World War II 2,600 Libyan Jews were sent to labor camps where 500 of them died. In the November 4, 1945 bloodbath "Arab nationalism and religious fanaticism in Tripoli was aimed at the physical destruction of the Jews" (p. 69). According to Clifton Daniel of the *New York Times*, "Many of the attacks were premeditated and coldly murderous (in) intent. Babies were beaten to death with iron bars. Old men were hacked to pieces where they fell. Expectant mothers were disemboweled, whole families were burned alive in their houses" (p. 69-70). There was forced conversion, girls raped with their families forced to watch. Only Jewish homes, businesses and persons were devastated. Of the 38,000 Jews in 1948, only 8,000 remained three years later. By 1960, only a few hundred remained, and they were forced to literally run for their lives. Most became a part of the 37,000-member Libyan refugee community in Israel.

With as much hatred as these Muslim countries have directed at the Jews over the centuries, one might think that they should be happy to have them out of their borders. But it is not enough that they are gone, apparently, they think they should also be dead. Because of the world wars, the Middle East's map lines were very fluid over the 20th century. Many regime leadership changes were taking place as well. The current nations of Syria, Iraq, Iran, etc. are not ancient nations who have invested in their lands from time immemorial as they purport. It was certainly not as if Israel was a newcomer infringing on Ancient Arab lands as has been propagandized to sway world media. When did the current nations of the Middle East form?

- Afghanistan 1919
- Algeria 1962
- Iraq 1932
- Iran 1979
- Jordan 1946
- Kuwait 1969 and liberated from Iraq in 1991
- Pakistan 1947
- Saudi Arabia 1927 and 1932 added territory

- Syria 1961
- United Arab Emirates 1971
- Yemen 1990
- Libya 1951, and replaced by a republic in 1969
- Lebanon 1926
- Morocco 1956
- Egypt 1922
- Turkey 1923

Proposed Population Exchange

As these nations were being formed and then recognized by the United Nations, they could have made room for their Arab brothers who lived in the newly re-formed nation of Israel. In fact many people recommended this as the solution. "In 1939, Mojli Amin, a member of the Arab Defense Committee of Palestine, drew up a proposal published in Damascus and distributed among Arab leaders entitled 'Exchange of Populations'" (p.25). The British proposed population exchange as well in 1947. Former U.S. President Herbert Hoover, stated in 1945, "The Arab population of Palestine would be the gainer from better lands in exchange for their present holdings. Iraq would be the gainer, for it badly needs agricultural population" (p.26). When 850,000 Jews left Arab countries and were settled into Israel's borders, these nations could have accepted one Arab refugee from Israel for every Jewish Arab they exiled and still come out to the good. Some nations such as Syria in 1951 were even encouraging the Arabs to come and receive land in exchange for working it. But the Arab leaders "rebuffed every effort to secure realistic well-being for their kinsmen" (p.23).

The leaders of the Arab world at a conference in Homs, Syria declared, "any discussion aimed at a solution of the Palestine problem which will not be based on ensuring the refugees' right to annihilate Israel will be regarded as a desecration to the Arab people and an act of treason" (p.23). Ralph Galloway neatly tied up everything while he was in Jordan in 1958 when he said in anger, "The Arab states do not want to solve the refugee problem. They want to keep it an open sore, as an affront to the United Nations, and as a weapon against Israel. Arab leaders do not give a damn whether Arab refugees live or die" (p.23).

> "The Arab states do not want to solve the refugee problem. They want to keep it an open sore, as an affront to the United Nations, and as a weapon against Israel."

Even King Hussein of Jordan stated two years later in 1960 as recorded by the Associated Press, "Since 1948 Arab leaders...have used the Palestine people for selfish political purposes. This is ridiculous and, I could even say, criminal" (p.23). These nations have refused the Arab refugees "because such measures would have terminated the refugees' status as refugees" (p.23). The refugees would have accepted their new homes and would not have desired to "return" to where they once lived in Israel.

Keep hanging in there, this is not as difficult as it sounds. It was not as if there had never been a population exchange before. From 1933 to 1945, 79.2 MILLION people were displaced. And since WWII another 100 MILLION people became refugees. Throughout history, when people feel threatened or insecure they have migrated to regions where they felt safe. It is considered normal by the world community. In "refugee exchanges there is no historical, moral or other basis for one-way repatriation" (p.26). For example, in the 1950's India and Pakistan exchanged 8.5 million Sikhs and Hindus from Pakistan for 6.5 million Muslims from India. In 1913 Turkey and Bulgaria exchanged equal populations of 1.3 million as part of a treaty agreement, but it was compulsory. In 1923, Turkey and Greece exchanged 1.25 million Greeks and .35 million Turks. Millions of people have been resettled! Why are Arabs forced to stay in Israel and be treated differently?

The Jewish refugees who fled persecution in their Middle Eastern countries were not offered any reparations from their original nations, and were not, in fact, even allowed to bring out their own possessions. According to the US Committee for Refugees (USCR) in 1981, if the

"600,000 Jewish refugees resettled from Arab countries...three decades ago...had broadcast the persecution of Jews and other minorities in the Arab countries...Arab demand for one-sided repatriation might be received today in a different, more even-handed and objective perspective" (p.31). The USCR also notes that "As we have seen, all those hapless peoples counted as 'refugees' were not in fact refugees: many were needy souls of other nationalities who found sustenance in the camps, and in the process became—and their children became—unwitting human weapons in a holy war that never ends" (p.31).

When Israel was given statehood in May 1948, the surrounding Arab nations had already made preparations to invade, to take the land for themselves, and to extinguish the Jews in doing so. "Arabs in Israel too were invited by their fellow Arabs...to leave while the 'invading' Arab armies would purge the land of Jews. The invading Arab governments were certain of a quick victory; leaders warned Arabs in Israel to run for their lives" (p.12-13). The Arab leaders promised that soon they would be able to return and confiscate the leftover Jewish property. According to the Arab-sponsored Institute for Palestine Studies in Beirut, 68% of the Arab refugees who left Israel in 1948 for other Arab nations, left without seeing an Israeli soldier. But then, "After the Arab's defeat in the 1948 war, their (the Arabs') position became confused: some Arab leaders demanded the 'return' of the 'expelled' refugees to their former homes despite the evidence that Arab leaders had called upon the Arabs to flee." (p.13). At the same time, Jews who lived in predominately Arab lands or newly formed nations, were so persecuted that many fled for their lives. They were forced to leave behind their homes, livelihoods, savings, and everything they owned. All was confiscated by Arab leaders or the Jews' former neighbors!

Al-Haytham Al-Ayubi, who was a prominent Arab-Palestinian strategist, in 1974 wrote when he analyzed the efficacy of Arab propaganda tactics, "The image of Israel as a weak nation surrounded by enemies seeking its annihilation evaporated [after 1967], to be replaced by the image of an aggressive nation challenging world opinion" (p.15). Al-Ayubi recommended 1. "sham peace talks" however giving no "state of peace," 2. moral pressure together with carefully-balanced military tension" and 3. "continual guerilla activities" to erode Israel's self-confidence because "loss of human life remains a sore point for the enemy" (p. 15). I would just like to point out from this quote that loss of human life *should* be a "sore point" for ALL humans, not something to be overcome, as seems to be this speaker's objective for exploitation.

Even up until the Six-Day War when Israel crushed the surrounding Arab nations, the "Palestine for Palestinians" cause was met by complacency and ignorance. The Arab leaders made a calculated move, motivated to propagandize the topic, when they deliberately changed their reference to these people from "Arab refugees" to "Palestinian refugees." The foundation for the claim of the "Palestinian problem" is "the popular perception that the Arabs are the *only* hapless refugees that were uprooted in 1948" (p.31).

Another problem that has surrounded this standoff is that the definition of the word "refugee" has been changed for the census in 1950. Official records by Arab census figures and from the League of Nations mandate, place the number of refugee Arabs in Israel between 430 and 650,000. Then numbers varied all over the place and "Arabs refused to allow official censuses to be completed among the refuges. Observers have deduced that the Arab purpose was to seek greater world attention through an exaggerated population figure" (p.17). According to UNRWA the slippery numbers from the Arab population was because refugees "eagerly report births...and reluctantly report deaths" (p.17). Also workers sent in by the UNRWA said they had difficulty distinguishing "ordinarily nomadic Bedouins and...unemployed or indigent local residents" from genuine refugees. It is estimated that the relief roll listing the refugees was inflated by as many as 100 thousand to begin with. In Lebanon alone, according to the 1959 journal *Al-Hayat*, "Of the 120,000 refugees who entered Lebanon, not more than 15,000 are still in camps"[91] awaiting repatriation. They had already been absorbed into the Lebanese population.

The Big Lie
So why was this population still receiving a hand out and the foreign Arab leaders demanding that they be given their homes back in Israel?

Because this is a made up problem. The Arabs want to crush the Jews and are using every means to do it, including blatant lies. Case in point: the current president of Iran, Mahmoud Ahmadinejad. In an address to the UN on Sept 18, 2008, he said, "The Holocaust is a lie, and the real holocaust is happening to the Palestinians" and on **May 8, 2008, Israel's 60th birthday,**

> "Those who think they can revive the stinking corpse of the usurping and fake Israeli regime by throwing a birthday party are seriously mistaken."

> "Today the reason for the Zionist regime's existence is questioned, and this regime is on its way to annihilation.... (Israel) has reached the end like a dead rat after being slapped by the Lebanese." (Remarks on Israel's Independence Day, as quoted by Iran's official IRNA news agency)

To sum up this whole horrible scenario that the Jews have been living for 2,000+ years, I heard a "settler" who was being interviewed on *Tuesday Night Live from Jerusalem* in their show[92] which aired on Jan 17, 2010 say,

> We've been on a long journey as a Jewish people. We've been through a lot. We need to, instead of focusing on current events, I think we need to focus on our roots, our histories and of course in the context of the Torah. Which is the central aspect of our identity..."
> Interviewer, "You are saying the crisis in the Middle East, the terrorists, the Hamas are being created because we don't know who we are?"
> "The Creator of the Universe is using these puppets. If we were to figure out some solution today to get rid of all the Palestinians, it wouldn't matter. God would bring another...as we see in the books of the Tenach, the Judges...if it wasn't one oppressor, it was another. And every time it was always there for the same reason. To help us come to a place of introspection and analyze where we're doing things wrong. Where our connection with our Creator is gone awry. Where it is mistaken, and from there, we have to make the correction."[92]

Brilliantly stated. Enough said.

CHAPTER 11
LESSON: ISRAEL'S MODERN WAR STORIES

Topics: Independence War 1948, 1968, 1973 (Yom Kippur), Lebanon I & II, Intifada I & II, rockets into S'derot, miracle stories, every day terror attacks, 2012 survey results.

1948-1949 War of Independence
When David ben Gurion declared the independence of new State of Israel on the evening of May 14-15, 1948, the on-going skirmishes around the former Palestine/British Mandate area escalated sharply. There were three main fronts that had to be manned with soldiers: Jerusalem, Haifa, and the Tel Aviv area including the road between Tel Aviv and Jerusalem. But every village in the entire country was exposed to threats and had to be defended.

Unfortunately, there were no trained military fighters, no real air force, no heavy artillery, hardly any light artillery guns, no ammunition to speak of. But there was a flag, an anthem, and a common cause as the soon-to-be-citizens of the minutes-new country of Israel fought for their right to exist! The Israeli arsenal consisted of 900 rifles, 700 light machine guns, and 200 medium machine guns with an ammunition supply of about three days, all of which had to be smuggled in during the pre-Israel days under the noses of the British Army, because to be Jewish and to be caught with a weapon was punishable by death! The men and women fighting were irregular fighters known as the *"Haganah"*[93] from which the Israeli Defense Forces (IDF) emerged. They were mostly workers who could be called upon to fire a weapon (provided there was a weapon to fire). The men and women who were as close to a standing army as the new country could form numbered approximately 15,000. They were called *"Palmach."* The air platoon consisted of 11 single engine piper cubs that looked more like crop dusters than an Israeli Air Force, and 20 Royal Air Force trained pilots. The naval company contained about 300 sailors some with Royal Navy experience, some with "illegal" immigrant-running experience and a few motor boats. There were also about 3-4,000 militant men who committed anti-British attacks for a number of years before and during the British pull-out; they were called the *"Irgun."*

This "mighty Israeli army" faced off against a man, Haj Amin el Husseini, who led the Arabs in Palestine and declared that his goal was to destroy the entire Jewish community or drive it into the sea. Does that sound familiar? It is the same rhetoric coming from Ahmadinejad today. Two particular forces of Arabs in Palestine-turned-Israel had been allowed to train and enforce the law alongside the British forces: The Arab Legion and the Transjordan Frontier Force. So they were not only British-trained military forces, but armed.

But that's not all! The Mufti of Jerusalem had two guerrilla forces, each 1,000 men in strength, with military training from the Germans during WWII; these men were backed by the extreme fanatical Moslem Brotherhood of Egypt. In addition to the inside-Israel's-borders military might, there was the military potential of the entire Arab world: Egypt (with hundreds of fighting aircraft), Syria, Iraq, Transjordan, and Lebanon, even contingents from the Saudi Arabian Army attached to the Egyptians for this fight. These armies were equipped with British and French artillery and armor. "They had ready access to arms, ammunition and spares."[93]

Yet…God had already decided and decreed the outcome. Israel was to have a place of her own in the world once more. It was a time bathed in blood and tears. But city by city was liberated and the Arab forces were pushed back to their own territories. Most of the skirmishes slowed down by early 1949 as each country began signing peace treaties with Israel. (February-Egypt; March-Lebanon; April-Jordan; July-Syria) But keep in mind that to a people who are encouraged to lie to the enemy when Jihad has been declared, a signature signifying peace is worth only the piece of paper it is written on. It is a temporary "cease fire" so they can reorganize.

The Road to Jerusalem
One of the most significant battles came early on in Israel's existence, beginning even before David ben Gurion declared independence. Jerusalem had been under siege, blocked off from receiving arms, food and medical supplies by a series of Arab villages, namely Latrun, and outposts lying along the road now known as Highway 1 which winds between Tel Aviv and Jerusalem through a deep cavern lined with craggy rock hills and cliffs for much of its 36 miles.

Since the Arabs occupied the high ground, anyone driving or walking along the road was a blaring target. There stands even now along the beautifully black-topped freeway a handful of rust-colored vehicle hulls which have been preserved where they were disabled by artillery fire. But many, many trucks, loaded with supplies for the starving families in the Jerusalem Old City and surrounding areas were destroy beyond preservation. That highway was the only way to get through, and it was impassable.

One night, a couple of guys had an idea to try to drive a jeep off-road and bypass Latrun through the rocky hills behind the cliff line that had been cleared for the road. Amazingly, a couple of guys in Jerusalem had the same idea the very same night! And they ended up meeting at a point between the two cities! (and not shooting each other!) After some excited realizations, they each returned to their base camps, and reported the news to their commanding officers. They began to smooth out the route stretch by stretch, working at night, and praying for moonless nights so that the dust their road-making kicked up did not give them away.

The soldiers called this road the "Burma Road," named after the road that was built by the allies between China and Burma in WWII. After working only about two weeks,

> On the night of May 31/June 1, after some improve-
> ments were made in the road, a second convoy set out
> for the Harel Brigade, under the command of "Raanana,"
> the Harel operations officer. The passengers frequently
> had to hand carry the supplies and push the vehicles
> over the rocks and pits, but the convoy eventually
> reached Harel, marking the unofficial breakthrough of
> the Burma Road.[94]

Over the next few days, Jerusalem was resupplied and saved. This was certainly not the end of the War of Independence, but just one of the early battles that was imperative that the Israelis win, and God came through miraculously for this newly formed nation of His people!

Sinai Campaign, 1956

Not even a decade after her independence, in 1956, Israel was pushed into another war. This one was on her southern border with Sinai. There had been little invasions on all sides of Israel in an on-going basis. Egypt got a new president, Nasser, when he overthrew King Farouk in 1952.[93] After making some deals with Czechoslovakia for arms and tanks, Egypt cut off Israel's access to her ports at the Red Sea. "In 100 hours, Israeli forces captured the Sinai desert and routed the Egyptian army. Under intense US pressure, Israel withdrew from Sinai the following year."[95] This offensive has been studied and lauded for its use of diversionary tactics. One of the main differences between the IDF and other nation's military strategies has shown up by this time in the daily incursions: The IDF commanders lead the raids, invasions, defenses, or attacks rather than falling to the back of the lines.

The 6-Day War, 1968

Between January and March of 1967 there were 270 "incidents" at Israel's borders, mostly from Syria. On April 7, when Syrian gunners fired on a farmer, Israel sent up some planes to shoot the gunners. The Syrians sent up a couple of MiGs and a dogfight ensued. The Israelis ended up chasing the Syrians all the way to Damascus! Then in May, Anwar Sadat came home from Moscow and fed the Syrians lies that Israel was mounting a huge border invasion that was going to take place in five days. Then Israel heard that Egyptian troops were being reinforced in the Sinai. Obviously tension escalated in the whole region!

Egypt demanded that the UNEF peacekeeping force that had been in place for 10 years be removed. The UN rolled over and rolled out a few days later! Egypt cut off the Gulf of Aqaba to Israeli ships and denied them access to Iraqi oil. Since the Gulf of Aqaba is international water, it was considered by the world to be an act of war. When condemned for their actions, Nasser (Egypt) said to the world press corps, "The existence of Israel is in itself an aggression...what happened in 1948 was an aggression – an aggression against the Palestinian people."

Jordan signed a mutual defense treaty with Egypt, and by the beginning of June 1967, Egypt had amassed

> 210,000 troops ready for deployment, with 100,000 of
> them with 930 tanks ready in the Sinai.... Syria had

63,000 troops and Jordan 55,000 – totaling 328,000 troops ready to fight Israel. The Arabs had twice the number of tanks compared to Israel (2,330 against 1000) and far more combat aircraft too (682 compared to Israel's 286); (t)hey had 1,845 armored personnel carriers compared to Israel's 1,500.[96]

If fully mobilized, Israel could call up 250,000 men and women, though the vast majority were civilian. But June 5th, Israel launched a surprise attack on the Egyptian air field, taking out the entire Egyptian Air Force. At the same time, Israel sent a message to Jordan, telling them that if they remained neutral, there would be no attacks on the West Bank. When Jordan called Egypt to confirm the attacks, Egypt flatly lied to their ally, denying the attack even took place, much less that their air force had been decimated! So Jordan launched an immediate multi-pronged attack on Israel,

- Civilian suburbs of Tel-Aviv were shelled by artillery;
- Israel's largest military airfield, Ramat David, was shelled;
- Jordanian warplanes attacked the central Israeli towns of Netanya and Kfar Sava;
- Thousands of mortar shells rained down on West Jerusalem hitting civilian locations indiscriminately, including the Hadassah Hospital and the Mount Zion Church;
- Israel's parliament building (the Knesset) and the Prime Minister's office, each in Israeli-controlled West Jerusalem, were targeted;
- 20 Israelis died in these attacks; 1000 were wounded. 900 buildings in West Jerusalem were damaged.
- "Jerusalem is totally engulfed in war..." reported the British Consul-General that morning.
- All this happened before Israel reacted militarily against Jordan, or moved at all into the West Bank.

NOTE: Israel's entry into the West Bank in June 1967 was not part of a premeditated Israeli plan for territorial expansion. Quite the opposite: Israel's own Defense Minister instructed the army not to fight the Jordanians, or move into the West Bank. That position only changed as a result of Jordan's disregard for Israeli appeals to avoid hostilities, and by its intensive bombardment of Israeli targets. Israel's entry into the West Bank was an act of self-defense. Its presence there originates as a result, not of Israeli aggression, but of Jordanian aggression.[96]

On June 7, 1967, a brigade of soldiers moved through the Jerusalem Old City and hung the Israeli flag at the Temple Mount. According to participants (as interviewed in *Against All Odds*)[97], the soldiers were so moved at having liberated Jerusalem after 1,800 years that even the non-religious men were praying at the Western foundational wall and after praying sang their national anthem *"Hatikva"* meaning "the hope." It was the first time the stones that Jesus had walked on and taught on had heard their new song of Hope that had been penned in 1878, yet sung in Jewish hearts since the beginning of the Diaspora. Here are the results:

> Israel was now in a much stronger position than it ever had been...the area controlled by Israel had increased some four-fold...Golan Heights...River Jordan (area) ...Sinai Desert, which included at its southernmost tip the strategically placed Straits of Tiran...The area included the oil fields...Most important of all, this vast wasteland provided an ideal buffer to guarantee Israel's security against any recurring threat from Egypt.[98]

The War of Attrition, 1967-1970

Unfortunately the security did not last long. Within three weeks of the cease fire, the first major incident occurred at the Suez Canal. This incursion began what is known as "The War of Attrition." These four years of incursions along three borders with Egypt, Jordan Valley area with the PLO and Syria and Lebanon areas brought "complete innovations in the history of warfare,"[98] but it was not given much world media attention.

During a 90-day cease fire President Nasser of Egypt died and was replaced by President Anwar el Sadat. Sadat talked peace while laying the groundwork for major operations in the Suez Canal area. He freed himself from any Russian oversight and began training his troops for invasion. But "Israel was lulled into a false sense of security. The

146

Egyptians' leadership did everything it could to encourage the Israelis in their preconceived notions so as to strengthen this sense of security."[98] The Egyptians and Israelis fished next to each other in the Red Sea until October 6, 1973.

Olympic Team Murdered in Munich, 1972

Yasser Arafat directed a team of Palestinian terrorists, clothed in track suits, to break into the Munich Olympic Village in the early morning hours of September 5, 1972. They murdered, or kidnapped-then-murdered, 11 members of the Israeli Olympic Team. Three of the terrorists were captured and held prisoner. On October 29, Palestinians hijacked a commercial Luftansa flight and demanded that the three Munich Killers be set free.

Germany released the killers and Golda Meir—then Prime Minister of Israel—set into motion a plan to bring justice to those terrorists. Mossad implemented the "Wrath of God" and over the next few years hunted them down and killed almost every person involved in the murders of Israel's Olympic team, even down to the planners. However, the mastermind is still free. Abu Daoud revealed his part in his autobiography. In 1999, Daoud was awarded the Palestinian Prize for Culture for this book.[99] On "January 24, 2000, the official newspaper of Yasir Arafat's Palestinian Authority (*Al-Hayat Al-Jadida*) urged Arab regimes to boycott the summer Olympic Games in Australia, because a moment of silence was planned at the start of the games in memory of the eleven Israeli athletes murdered by Arafat's PLO terrorists at the 1972 Munich Olympics."[99]

Yom Kippur War, October 1973

On the holiest day of the year for Jews, when all is quiet throughout the entire land, no cars are operating, not even taxis, no purchases are made, not even food, the Israelis, when both soldiers and civilians were worshipping and praying in their synagogues, while Israel was reciting the ancient texts, enemy troops that had been amassing for a couple of days at the borders in "exercises" began their invasion.

One of the largest standing armies in the world, Egypt, which included 880,000 troops, 2,200 tanks, 2,300 artillery pieces, 150 anti-aircraft missile batteries, and 550 first-line aircraft, [98] came at Israel with their full might! "In the first minute of the attack, 10,500 shells fell on Israeli positions at the rate of 175 shells per second."[98] The Egyptians crossed the canal as the shells fell. "Initial Egyptian estimates had been that the crossing would cost some 25,000-30,000 (Israeli) casualties, including some 10,000 dead,"[98] however much to their surprise, only 208 were killed. There were 14 helicopters filled with Egyptian commandos that were shot down by Israeli Air Forces!

However, Israel still did not have a clear picture of the canal border until October 7th. It was becoming a slaughter as the brave, vastly out-numbered Israeli troops began to melt away. And the other borders were looking just as grim. The Israeli soldiers were fighting well, but there just was not enough military might behind them.

But God knew, and had pre-planned for some unexpected help.

U.S. President Nixon fulfills his destiny

In the United States, Henry Kissinger was the Secretary of State and advised President Nixon against helping Israel in the war, even though Israel asked for supplies. Kissinger said, "Let Israel bleed a little."[100] According to Lars Klein, Israel ran out of munitions in this fight for survival.[101] However, Golda Meir, Israel's Prime Minister at the time, called President Nixon's private line at 3 A.M. Washington D.C. time. She begged him for help.

And what makes this midnight plea for help even more interesting is that, according to McKay's, *Against All Odds,*

> as Nixon sat on the side of his bed, listening to Golda Meir's request over the phone, instead of hearing the Prime Minister's voice, he heard the voice of his mother....as a young boy growing up, his mother had told him that one day he would be in a powerful position, and a situation would arise where Israel and the Jews needed his help. When it did, he was to help them.[102]

Nixon over-nighted an arsenal to Israel! And the IDF rallied and won the Yom Kippur War in days. (Best use of over-night "mail" service I have ever heard!) While Nixon had tons of problems with his presidency, I believe that God used him as an Esther, "for such a time as this" to save the Jewish people. And therefore, he fulfilled his destiny.

Lebanon I & II Wars (1978 - 2000, heavy in 1982) and (2006) Very briefly.

The First Lebanon War lasted for 22 years with skirmishes back and forth across borders as Israel tried to keep her border towns from being attacked. It began in 1978 when PLO terrorists invaded Israel and murdered an American tourist walking on the beach, then they hijacked a bus. When Israelis intercepted the bus, the terrorists opened fire, killing 34 people.[103] The IDF then invaded Lebanon to push the terrorists back from the border. They withdrew two months later so that the UN could patrol and monitor the border. That didn't go so well because the UN was not strong enough to prevent arms or terrorists from infiltrating Lebanon. Israeli leaders in Jerusalem constantly reiterated that they did want not one inch of Lebanese land, they just wanted peace, which after 22 years when the IDF finally exfiltrated, they were able to prove.

The Second Lebanon War began to charge the atmosphere on my second day in Israel in the summer of 2006. Two IDF soldiers were kidnapped when Hezbollah militants fired rockets across the border as a diversion for an anti-tank missile attack on two Israeli humvees on border patrol. Five soldiers were killed. Five more were killed in a failed rescue attempt. Israel responded with air attacks on Lebanese infrastructure including highways and bridges that allowed resupplying of Hezbollah with armaments. Then the rockets started flying. More than 100 per day fell on Israel's cities in the north. The residents of many of those cities, including Israel's third largest city Haifa, fled to more southern cities such as Tel Aviv and Jerusalem. The IDF launched a ground invasion and a naval blockade. The conflict lasted 34 days and most IDF troops withdrew from Lebanon by October 1, 2006.

On July 16, 2008, almost two years later, the kidnapped soldiers' bodies were exchanged for "incarcerated Palestine Liberation Front militant Samir Kuntar, who was convicted of murder in Israel, four Hezbollah militants, and bodies of about 200 other Lebanese and Palestinian militants captured by Israel."[104]

Intifada I & II (Dec 1987-1993) and (2000-2003)
These are two time periods when terrorism became an almost-daily event inside populated cities and along the roadsides of Israel. The **First Intifada** manifested mostly as rock throwing with a goal of throwing off the Jewish "occupiers." In the **Second Intifada** the goal of the terrorists was different. They already had a lot of autonomy, governing themselves and providing their own security in the West Bank and Gaza. They were trying to strengthen their political position with Israel.[98] Terrorists would sneak outside the towns where they lived loaded with explosives (with an endless supply from the surrounding nations) and find a "soft target," meaning someplace with lots of people to blow up. Pizza parlors, shopping malls, buses taking people to work, school and shopping, kindergartens, grocery stores, and embassies were bombed, murders occurred in roadside ambushes, and while driving, even home invasions. March 26, 2001, even a baby carriage was not a safe haven. Ten-month-old baby Shalhevet was shot in the head by a sniper while her parents were strolling her to visit her grandparents in Hebron.[105]

The security fence that was built around the Gaza Strip before the IDF and the Israelis left, and the fences that have been built around cities such as Bethlehem and Jericho, are much debated both outside and inside Israel. But results cannot be argued with:

> All in all the Gaza Strip saw more than 50 per cent of the total Palestinian attacks (9,600) during the three years of the *intifada*, with only 10 per cent of the Israeli casualties. In contrast to Gaza, terrorists from the West Bank succeeded in penetrating Israeli city centers with astonishing ease.[106]

After more debate, the construction of concrete walls has commenced to surround the West Bank to keep the number of terrorist successes as low as possible. So on a day to day basis, even now, the security level is high. Every bus station, shopping center and little store or sidewalk café has a security guard to check your bags and purses for any suspicious devices. The interrogations and 6 to 9 levels of security checks (that *I've* seen, which means there are probably more!) at Ben Gurion International

Airport are legendary! The specialized terrorist police are top notch in Jerusalem especially. They ride around two to a motorcycle all dressed in black. The huge guy in front drives in and out of vehicle traffic or foot-traffic quick as a wink, while the huge guy on the back holds a really big gun! They have developed specialized bomb squads that cordon off the road when a suspicious package is left unattended, and the little robots are sent in to detonate it. (P.S. There is no lost & found in Israel. Don't forget your purse/briefcase on a bus. ...it will be blown up and traffic diverted!) and when the bomb squad does not arrive in time, a specialized unit of men and women who have way too much experience are called in to clean up the results and take care of the body parts for an under-24-hours-required funeral. However it usually is traffic-back-to-normal within a couple of hours.

Daily Rockets in Sderot
Just a few kilometers inside the Israel border near the Gaza Strip (land that belonged to Israel as spoils of war but they gave up so the Arabs who call themselves Palestinians could have a place of their own rule) is a town called Sderot. On a daily basis for years now, rockets are hurled from Gaza into this town. Children are so terrorized that they will take a one hour walk to school instead of the 20 minute walk because of the number of bomb shelters available on either route. The residents of Sderot have about 15-18 seconds when the siren sounds to jump up from school, work or play, or sleep to hide themselves in the reinforced bomb shelters. Every family is affected.

The people cannot move. First, it is the principle of being terrorized to leave your home. Secondly, the housing market is about zero! They are locked into mortgages and can't afford to move. But they also are held captive from fighting back.

The Sderot police department keeps the empty, twisted shells on display on racks out back.

And the world says "poor Palestinians." On occasion, with specific intel, the IDF will launch counterattacks and take out terrorists who hide behind the *hijabs* and *abayas* (skirts and veils) of their women and videos of their band-aided children.

151

This is not last decade or even a few years ago. This happens everyday in Sderot! Today. Maybe right this second. Please take a moment to pray for safety and relief for the residents of Sderot.

Miracles take place in Israel, especially during wartime. One of my favorite stories occurred during the Yom Kippur War.

In the Golan Heights, on the Syrian Border, one night in October 1973, IDF soldiers entered a huge minefield that they were well into before they realized they were surrounded by live mines. They had to get to the other side, and there was no going around. Being in a live mine field, it was just as dangerous to turn back! Using their bayonets, detached from their weapons of course, the soldiers kneeled over to begin sifting the sand a few inches at a time to located the mines and make their way through. It could take weeks, step by step, to make it safely across!

Quote too good to leave out: "The military academy of West Point won't study Israel's wars because the outcomes are too impossible!" –Michael Greenspan [107]

They managed to expose a few mines and dismantle them when suddenly, a "very, very strong gust of wind came." The wind storm tossed dust, sand and grit high into the air. Visibility became almost non existent. The soldiers hunkered down protecting their faces and fought to breathe against the flying sand. As suddenly as it came, the wind disappeared. When the soldiers rose up, they were in awe. The wind had blown away the sand that was hiding thousands and thousands of mines sprinkled throughout the huge field. All of the danger had been exposed, and they walked though with out a scratch (or "even the smell of smoke", as described in Daniel about Shadrach, Meshach and Abed-Nego in the Fiery Furnace!)

David Yaniv, now a veteran tank commander from the Yom Kippur War relayed this event he experienced to Jewish-American reporter Michael Greenspan in an interview recorded in the *Against All Odds* series. Some of the mines had been buried 25 to 30 centimeters deep (9.5 to 12 inches). The minute the mines were exposed, the wind stopped.[107] This event reminds me of the miracles of ancient Israel.

The Picture Presented to the World when Israel is at War

One thing which must be grasped when we talk about Israel's wars, both ancient and modern, is not whether God is on Israel's side, fighting against Israel's enemies. Because Israel is God's special possession, nations who do not receive her as such can bring about their own enmity with God, but it is not merely because nations hate Israel, it is that by hating Israel, they are hating God Himself and are acting in rebellion to His plan, which is the same as walking in-line with Satan's will (to steal, kill and destroy) and to take that which belongs to the Father (our worship and our selves for eternity). Israel's outcome in war boils down to whether Israel is on God's side.

There were plenty of ancient wars when Israel suffered slaughter because they were not on God's side, in fact in those times they were squarely against Him and not keeping the covenant they made with Him. Ancient Canaan was against God and doing detestable things, and God used Israel to root out the evil among them. Then God used Nebuchadnezzar to squash the ancient Israelites, not to extinction but to a point of realization that they were dependant on God, who was also their Covenant counterpart. Hard times invite people to turn to God for help, for relationship.

God's desire has always been for fellowship with mankind. It is why we were created in the first place. After sin entered into the world though, we could not fellowship with God for His holiness would kill us. That is why he chose a people (Israel) who could chase after holiness in the provision He made for them that the blood of lambs and goats would suffice to cover their sins until He put more permanent measures of forgiveness, cleansing and holiness in place (Jesus). God chose them to be a picture of His holiness to hold up for the world to see and desire to become people who are holy, separate unto God. So far, this is still a coming time. But rest assured. It is coming!

God has a plan that He is enacting. Israel is a part of His plan and His plan is for them (to become His beautiful counterpart and Bride in holiness). While Israel is the chosen one to display a picture of God's holiness, they are at the same time being invited into His heart.

Think of it as a theater play. God as the author and producer presents Himself in the person of Jesus to the world as a way to be reconciled to the Almighty Creator. While He uses the Jews and the Church as "characters" in His "play" they are also being presented with the message of the play at the same time. The message: I love you and desire that "all Israel may be saved" (Rom 11:26) that the whole world accept Jesus' salvation. He actually blinded His own Chosen People for a time (until the full number of Gentiles has come in—Rom 11:25). Revelation 6:11 also alludes to this idea that God is delaying His return until the "full number" of people are His. He doesn't want to lose even one. They are both what the play is about and who the play is for.

The war over people's hearts individually and a nation of hearts is just that: God is fighting for people's heart. Sometimes this war in the spirit breaks out in the natural with violence.

It is my opinion that Israel is in a precarious position in her history right now. They are a nation which in general is secular, apart from God, and not holy. Even with all of the miracles that have occurred in her rebirth, Israel has not as a nation set her face toward God. They are without question a primary part of God's plan and have been a sword used by God against people and nations who are NOT lined up with God plan of redemption right now (referring to the Arabs who are fighting Israel's rebirth and settling in the Land God gave them forever). God does not wish that any (ANY! Neither Israel nor Gentiles rebelling against Him) should perish, but that all would turn to Him. (paraphrasing I Timothy 2:4, II Peter 3:9).

2012 Survey Stats by Guttman-Avi Chai [108]
80% of Israeli Jews believe that God exists
70% of respondents believe the Jews are the Chosen People,
65% believe the Torah is God-given
56% believe in life after death
37% of Israeli Jews had a problem with fellow Jews not following the biblical commandments
Nearly 70% wanted more entertainment venues open on Shabbat. These numbers, however, coincide with other recent findings that Israelis are increasingly hungry for a deeper spiritual life. [109]

CHAPTER 12
LESSON: MODERN ISRAELI CULTURE

Topics: What is it like to live in Modern Israel, population, Nobel Prize winners, the plight of Messianic Jews, current worship in Christian congregations

Let me first dispel the ancient images you might have of Jerusalem being a large collection of little stone huts with dusty people walking around in sandals, robes and turbans, leading camels or donkeys down narrow dirt paths. Jerusalem is as "first-world" in its dress and technology as any city in America. There are not as many tall glass and steel buildings as New York or Chicago, but there are some, mostly in Tel-Aviv and Haifa. In Jerusalem, the building codes do not allow buildings to be taller than the temple will be when it is rebuilt, and all buildings must be built with (or have a façade of) white Jerusalem stone that is finished with a chipped limestone look.

You are more likely to see some crazy combination of American and European style clothing and really weird foot gear (though I did come across some nice boots and flip flop styles!) than robes and turbans (but there are some of those too!). The Ultra Orthodox Jewish men dress in their circa 1940's three-piece black suits and hats at all times and their wives are predominantly wearing longish black skirts in tons of varied styles and long-sleeved black or white tops and sturdy dark shoes with a scarf over their hair or a chin-length wig that covers their hair. Everyone else is sporting an "anything-goes" style. There are nuns and priests living there from virtually every denomination that has nuns and priests. So, they are running around town in their various outfits.

Everyone in Israel has their cell phone or texting phone just like America. And service is unusually good. Wi-fi is available virtually anywhere. And on Ben Yahuda Street, (remember him? The man who pushed for Hebrew language) the main tourist shopping area, wi-fi access is free. There are smoothies made from the freshest of fruits while you watch. Coffee shops, bakeries, grocery stores, pharmacies, and boutique clothing stores, big movie theaters with release dates usually just a week or so behind American schedules, churches, synagogues, mosques, mammoth museums, green parks, soccer stadiums, shopping malls, and traffic jams. It is very much like America except on a compact scale, and of course, the security guard (and/or metal detector) that checks your bags before you enter any store. People in Jerusalem, like most cities, do a lot of walking or taking the bus wherever they need to go, because it is a lot cheaper and less hassle than trying to drive in crazy-man traffic with the busses and taxis or find parking.

Hospitals are modern except in that they send their patients home over Shabbat...weird. All the doctors and nurses are off, so unless someone is on life support or pretty close to it, they go home on Friday afternoon and come back to the hospital on Sunday morning.

There are still Kibbutzim where people live collectively on farm-type land, but they generally have some sort of tourist trade, whether a restaurant, B&B, fresh produce, or a product factory of some sort. And yes, they have their cell phones, cable TV, and internet out there too.

There are amazing 5-star hotels and eateries in almost every city, especially the coastal cities. All pilgrims to the Land should not leave without having at least one full Israeli breakfast, including tons of different salads (cucumbers, tomatoes, lettuces, peppers of all colors, onions, salsas) delicious yogurts, pastries, fruits—peeled or whole, breads, they even set out eggs (for the American tourists!) but everything is dairy, no meat for breakfast to keep the kitchen kosher.

Population
So who makes up the population of Israel? We already know that **Jews** from around the world have made aliyah to Israel. There are major populations of Russian Jews, and Ethiopian Jews are on the rise. Many of the Jews who remained in Europe after the Holocaust, called "Survivors," moved to Israel. There are families who immigrated from Muslim nations in the Middle East too. And a few Americans. People born in Israel and raised there are called *Sabre* (saw'-brugh) which is translated "cactus." It is an excellent personality description. They can be so prickly and loud and sometimes obnoxious on the outside, but if you make a friend and get to see their soft, sweet inside, you have a friend for life. And, I assume, that the prickly outside is a protection mechanism learned through the generations of persecution.

156

Besides the Jews though, there are **Christians** from nearly every denomination and country who have formed communities in cities throughout Israel. Most are there on short-term volunteer visas or clergy visas. Some have been granted long-term volunteer visas or work visas. But to virtually every Christian whom the Lord has granted the privilege of living in Israel, it becomes "home" forever. There is ever a longing to return.

There are **Arabs**, both Christian and Muslim in religion, who live in Israel, and they do have a hard time of it. Jobs are hard to come by, except on Saturday when all the Jews are not working and need to be served.

There are communities of **Druze**. Not Jews; not Druids. The Druze have their own separate religion and court jurisdiction. They are peace-loving and give loyalty to whomever is in control of the government of the land where they live. These hundred thousand citizens are Arab by culture and language, and they serve in the IDF.[110]

There is a contingent of about 3,000 **Armenians,** half of whom live in Jerusalem. They are Christians who immigrated to Israel to be near the Upper Room around the turn of the first millennium. After the Armenian Holocaust of 1915 in which 1 to 1.5 million Armenians were murdered in Turkey, some survivors made their way to Israel.[111] The Armenians are the only minority in Israel to teach their children the Hebrew language in their own schools.[112]

Throughout the Land of Israel in arid places in the Negev and even right outside Jerusalem, **Bedouins** make their camps and tend their goats and camels, living in tents and makeshift "houses" of tin and wood scraps. One of the funniest things I ever saw in Israel was while I was driving on a beautiful, newly paved road outside Jerusalem on the way to the Dead Sea. It was super hot outside and walking atop a rocky, barren hill was a Bedouin dressed in long, heavy black robes and a *keffiyeh* (checkered Arab head scarf). His robes fluttered slightly in a blast of hot breeze up from the desert. He was leading a camel by a rope, and he was talking away…on his cell phone! Ancient meets modern, and this is Israel!

The Plight of Messianic Jews

A Messianic Jew, or a "completed Jew" is what a person is called who was born Jewish, by blood and/or religion and who believes that Jesus (Yeshua) is the promised Messiah who was God in the form of a man who died and was raised back to life and is now seated at the right hand of God. Life is doubly hard for these men, women and families. While they do have the joy of knowing both Judaism and Christianity and the depth that combination gives to God's Word, most do not feel accepted by either religion. Beyond that, Messianic Jews in Israel especially are persecuted, many times even by their own families. The families use the full power of their persuasive techniques and sometimes resort to threats or violence. But when that does not convince the new believer in Yeshua back to Jewish traditions, they cut the person off. Even to the point of holding a funeral and sitting *shiva* (mourning for 7 days), and the believer is then "dead" to the family, and they never speak to them again! On occasion, the Israeli government will even revoke citizenship of new *olim* (new immigrants) who "claimed to be Jewish" and then are found to be "Christian." A Messianic Jew that I know in Israel who prefers to remain anonymous told me that when his neighbors found out that he believed in Yeshua, they refused to speak to him or even look at him any more, and they made inflammatory comments about him to others within his hearing.

> (T)he mindset of those who are persecuting the Messianic Jews of Israel believe themselves to be defending Jews from "missionaries" who are "stealing the souls of Jews." Some consider the Jews who believe in Jesus to be more dangerous than Hamas terrorists.... Most Israeli Messianics keep the proverbial stiff upper lip when it comes to the persecution and threats they often experience. They are mindful not to stir up anti-Semitic sentiment by communicating what is going on with them in the Jewish homeland. The believers in Israel are living examples of the Sermon on the Mount, walking circumspectly regarding persecution, by turning the other cheek and forgiving those that persecute and abuse them.[113]

While I lived in Israel in 2007-08, there was a young Messianic teenager, Ami Ortiz, who received at his front door a basket of food and goodies for his family to celebrate Purim. When he opened it, it was a bomb that blew him and his family's home apart. Even windows on the cars on the street were blown out by the impact. Miraculously, Ami survived. His story hit the internet and believers all over the world united in prayer for his restoration. Over the next year, he endured many surgeries, and heart ache, but the Lord brought him back to wholeness. The bombing was hardly even investigated after initial reports showed that it was likely that a segment of ultra orthodox Jews had sent it because of the family's leadership in a Messianic congregation in Ariel, Israel.

There are now Messianic Synagogues throughout Israel and the world to be a support system in religion, family life, and community. Many of the larger US cities have congregations of Messianic believers. (They usually welcome gentiles as well!)

Church Services in Jerusalem
I have attended several different churches in Jerusalem, though by no means all of the Christian believers' gatherings. Some congregations meet on Friday night, some on Saturday morning or evening, some on Sunday evening. They are generally called "congregations" because of the bad connotations left by the word "church" to the Jews.

The one I attended most regularly would begin with the "Shma" (words shown in lesson one) being sung a cappella in Hebrew. The words in Hebrew & English transliteration were projected overhead with nice modern graphics behind them. Then the worship band and vocalists would lead some fast and some slow songs in English and/or Hebrew for about 30 minutes. Then there was a time of greeting each other during the transition. (Inevitably each week, everyone would be asked to scoot into the middle of the rows, as they were very long theater-type rows for seating, so that there was room for late-comers.) There was some announcements of coming events to participate in and pray for, followed by a report from the prayer room. The children were then blessed and dismissed to their classes, and then the Torah Portion for the week (Torah Portions are described in the birthday section of chapter 14) was taught/shared by a different man or woman each week for about 10 minutes. The pastor then usually gave a message for about 30-40 minutes. It was normally more relevant to those who are serving in fulltime ministry capacity since they and persecuted Jewish believers made up most of the congregation, (as opposed to new believers or the unchurched). They normally wrapped up with a couple more songs, individual prayer ministry, and an invitation to continue worshiping in the 24-hour prayer rooms if you so desired.

The 2- to 2.5-hour services run a little longer than the average 1- to 1.5-hour services in the U.S. Congregations usually offer opportunities to lead or attend discipleship small groups during the week too.

CHAPTER 13
THE COVENANT GOD OF A COVENANT PEOPLE.

Topics: Creation Covenant, what is Covenant? Abrahamic, Mosaic, Jesus, Communion

Most people believe that the covenant between Abraham and God was the first covenant made, but Genesis 8 records a pre-Abrahamic covenant of God with creation. It takes place after the Flood, which cleansed the earth from the filth that had been growing exceedingly worse with every generation.

God's Covenant with Creation
Only 10 generations (Gen 5:3-29) passed from Adam who lived in the Garden of Eden in perfection with his Creator, to Noah, whose generation was so unrighteous that God had to destroy it. Gen 6:5-7

> Then the Lord saw that the wickedness of man was great in the earth and that every intent of the thoughts of his heart was only evil continually. And the Lord was sorry that He had made man on earth, and He was grieved in His heart. So the Lord said, "I will destroy man whom I have created from the face of the earth, both man and beast, creeping thing, and birds of the air, for I am sorry I have made them."

Creation suffered because of man's sin in the garden and the growth of evil in man's heart. Sin does not effect only the one sinning, but every sin touches every person in the world, and in the future, and even the earth itself, and creation, and the God who made it all. Can you feel the emotion of God's heart when describes that he was sorry and grieved that He had made man? It had only been 10 generations since God had enjoyed perfect fellowship in the Garden with the man he created. His heart was still crying out for fellowship with man. It was why God had created man. In all his creations God had created part and counterpart. But man, God made in His own image, as a counterpart for Himself. Eve came about as a companion for Adam, so that he would not be alone. She came out of Adam. She had once been contained in Adam's heart (or side, if you like) and God separated a part of him and called that part woman.

The LORD God said, "It is not good for the man to be alone. I will make a helper suitable for him." Now the LORD God had formed out of the ground all the beasts of the field and all the birds of the air. He brought them to the man to see what he would name them; and whatever the man called each living creature, that was its name. So the man gave names to all the livestock, the birds of the air and all the beasts of the field.

But for Adam no suitable helper was found. So the LORD God caused the man to fall into a deep sleep; and while he was sleeping, he took one of the man's ribs and closed up the place with flesh. Then the LORD God made a woman from the rib he had taken out of the man, and he brought her to the man.

The man said, "This is now bone of my bones and flesh of my flesh; she shall be called 'woman,' for she was taken out of man." Gen 2:18-23

But God's counterpart had utterly turned away from Him and no longer desired His presence. Man had been created to worship though, and there was no way to live without worshiping, so man rejected His creator, the part of His counterpart-ed-ness, and made for himself his own gods to worship. So God's heart was disappointed, but not only that, but the stench of sin was so potent on earth that it raised to heaven. And God could not let it continue. So He found a man righteous, or perfect in all his generations in Noah (Gen 6:9). God asked him to build an ark so that God could start over from the righteous seed that He had found in Noah. After the destruction, it is almost like God is brooding over the earth again like He did when He was creating it. The first thing Noah did when vacating the ark was build an altar and sacrifice (from his very limited supply, I might add as an aside) in worship to the one true God.

And the Lord smelled a soothing aroma! (Gen 8:20-22).

Then Noah built an altar to the LORD and, taking some of all the clean animals and clean birds, he sacrificed burnt offerings on it. The LORD smelled the pleasing aroma and said in his heart: "Never again will I curse the ground because of man, even though every inclination of his heart is evil from childhood. And never again will I destroy all living creatures, as I have done. "As long as the earth endures, seedtime and harvest, cold and heat, summer and winter, day and night will never cease."

And the Lord made a covenant with Noah and every living creature (and therein their perpetual generations) that He would never again destroy all flesh by flood waters. He set the rainbow in the clouds as a sign of that covenant.

Now Noah didn't have to ask, because ancient peoples knew what a covenant was. Today the definition and implications are less clear.

What is a covenant?

A covenant goes beyond a "treaty" or "pact" drawn up between two parties, whether they be individuals or two peoples or two (or more) nations. A covenant is a designed relationship of inter-dependence. When a covenant is between individuals, the people are usually equals. However, in groups or nations, one party is usually greater and one is lesser in the agreement. The one that is greater is the one that has responsibility to draw up the terms of the agreement. The lesser party has the right to refuse the covenant's terms (but they end up living in conflict with the greater if they reject the offer, such as when a conquering king descends into a land.). In Africa, even today, a covenant is an agreement that can never be broken. It is not just legally binding, it obligates the soul to fulfill the contract even if it costs one's own death.

A covenant is recorded, both parties receive a copy. It is re-read often.

Even though our English Bibles translate that covenants are "made" between people, a more accurate term should refer to covenants as "being cut." They were yucky, bloody messes. Animals were slaughtered as the covenants were being cut to remind both parties that they could expect death as a penalty of breaking covenant. It is the most serious agreement in the world and cannot be revoked.

It is a huge deal that God as the greater party (obviously) obligated Himself to man through a covenant. Even more amazing is the second covenant with man.[114]

Abrahamic Covenant
Even though after the Flood man's lifetime was shortened to a 120 years maximum, sin still grew rampant on the earth in just a short time (about 350 years!) which, incidentally, was another 10 generations. God again missed the fellowship that He had enjoyed with Adam and Noah, and a few others along the way.

God deeply desired a "breed" of man who would worship Him as the counterpart who had been lost twice to this point in His Story. A people with whom He could share life and His heart. He wanted to be chosen. To be loved. To be known. God's heart was overflowing with this deep love He had for the man he had made, but there was no one who was willing to be lavished with love.

So God searched for a man who could be a righteous man, a man who would believe in Him. And God found Abram, an idol maker in Ur of the Chaldees. When God called Abram to leave his home and follow Him, Abram did! God's heart leapt in delight. (Songs 4:9 You have stolen my heart with one glance of your eyes) "Someone said yes! Someone wants me. This man is willing to be loved!" God must have thought.

Since we have already talked about the promises God made to Abraham (and fulfilled!) we will skip ahead to ask, what was God up to with these promises to make a great nation from this man who couldn't seem to have a single son on his own in the first 86 years of his life?

He was after a people He could call His own: a People who would represent holiness and right relationship between God and man to the rest of the world. This Ultimate Plan God has is to provoke jealousy among the nations and cause them to turn to Him. He wants His counterpart back!

The Covenant between Abraham and God is recorded in Genesis 15. It is to be re-read often. God promised Abram a son of his own body that would become a nation as numerous as the stars and the Land from the river of Egypt to the Euphrates River. When Abram asked for confirmation of this inheritance, God called for a 3-year-old heifer, a 3-year-old female goat, a 3-year-old ram, a turtledove and a young pigeon. After Abram prepared the animals by chopping each of the four large animals in half, head to tail, God put him in a deep sleep. God appeared as a smoking oven and a flaming torch and passed between the pieces of dead, bloody flesh. Thus obligating Himself, as the greater party, even unto His own death, to fulfill the covenant. Never had a "god" obligated himself to relationship with man before. It was unthinkable to the pagan mind.

A while later, God renewed His covenant with Abram (after the whole Ishmael debacle). And as a sign of the covenant God required that all the males in Abram's family be circumcised (got some blood involved there too!). Abram and Sarai received new names. Shortly thereafter, the promised son was conceived and delivered! And God set into motion the whole plan for having a people who were after His heart, a counterpart to Himself!

Four generations later when worship of Jehovah and communion with God had been established in the hearts of Abraham's family, (though they made their share of mistakes and intentional sin along the way) the Hebrews (numbering 70ish by this time) moved to Egypt. They became enslaved for 400 years, until the appointed hour when Moses was raised up to lead them home to the Promised Land.

Mosaic Covenant

Three months into the desert journey the Israelites reached Mount Sinai, where God met with Moses and the people. He offered to renew covenant with them as Abraham's children. He said, "You have seen what I did to the Egyptians, and how I bore you up on eagles' wings and brought you to myself. Now, therefore, if you will indeed obey my voice and keep my covenant, then you shall be a special treasure to Me above all people, all the earth is mine. And you shall be to be a kingdom of priests and a holy nation."

After Israel took three days to get ready for a meeting with a holy God, God spoke the Ten Commandments. Freaked the Israelites out! They were afraid they wanted Moses to talk to God and tell them what He said. So Moses agreed and the 10 commands became 613 laws to govern their lives as a holy people, set apart from other nations.

God laid out in the covenant (written down in the Torah) the blessings with which He would bless them if they followed the covenant, and the curses that would befall them if they broke covenant. And then He asked Israel if they wanted His terms of covenant. They said they wanted the covenant.

> Exodus 19:8 The people all responded together, "We will do everything the LORD has said." So Moses brought their answer back to the LORD.

And the Lord finally had a people who belonged to Him, but in name only. They promised to keep the Law, but He was after their hearts, and they were very afraid of Him!

And all this time since, in all their generations, the Israelites have been trying to keep the (impossible) law, all the while, God pursues their hearts. He called them away to dwell with Him, to rest in His love. And they are so focused on not breaking the covenant, they have missed that the God of the universe is wooing and desiring their hearts, that the covenant has been updated again already. The demand for a blood payment for original sin (and ALL sin from that moment forward) has come and the greater party of the covenant laid down the full and perfect price.

The price: Jesus, God Himself, paying the death and blood price. How extravagant is the love of God. He gave Himself to reconcile His counterpart unto Himself.

The Covenant of Jesus (New Covenant)
The Covenant of Jesus is fulfillment of all that the Law was. Where the Law exposed sin, by giving a list of dos and don'ts, the new covenant of Jesus gives permanent resolution to that exposed sin.

A trend that I have noticed among Christians is to use the phrase "We are no longer under the law." However where knowledge is lacking, foolishness abounds. Most importantly, the scripture actually says: We are not under the CURSE of the Law. That does not mean the Law is a curse, but the curses associated with breaking the Law (as in blessings and curses) we can be free from.* The old covenants did not disappear. God did not give the law just to be mean. Every law and principle He gave was out of love. Now, 3,500 year later we can see, scientifically, the outcome of living by these laws brings longevity, or "life more abundant." Hand washing, skin infection care, clean and unclean animals to eat, abstinence before marriage, faithfulness in marriage, keeping the Sabbath a day of rest, God even provided instruction for proper handling of waste and corpses. These laws were designed by a loving Father who was explaining to His children how to live well within the world He had created. He knew the laws because He had put them in place. The laws came with blessings and curses for those who obeyed or disobeyed.

All of those principles are still in place and we will do well if we follow them. The difference now is that when we disobey the law, if we have entered into the new covenant, with Jesus being the payment for our disobedience, we are given grace because Jesus paid our debt for us. Jesus was sent to earth, lived a blameless (sin free) life and then gave His life as the payment for all the sins of man, just as the lamb had represented in the earlier covenant.

However, this covenant is like the others in that it is two sided, one party being the greater and one the lesser, but it still costs both parties. And it costs us more on the human side than the old covenant did. Just as it cost God more. (His only Son's life).

The New Covenant costs the individual more than just "do not commit adultery." Jesus said if you look with lust upon a woman it is the same as having had the affair with her in your heart. OK, that is more man oriented, but ladies, what do you think the Lord thinks about reading romanticized trashy novels or movies. That fills a lady's heart with lust and unfulfillable expectations. And what about idolatry? The Original Covenant says we shall have no other gods before the one true God. In the New Covenant that costs us more than just not bowing before ba'al or molech, God wants us to lay down anything that has more pull or influence our hearts more than He does.

The cost of the New Covenant is our hearts, not merely adhering to a list of rules. Following those rules though, honors the way God made the world and helps us to fulfill the New Covenant terms we agreed to.

The benefits of the New Covenant far outweigh the cost: We get to know God, to enter into His presence without fear, we get to partner with Him in bringing His kingdom to earth as is it is heaven, we get to know that our names are written in the Lamb's Book of Life guaranteeing us eternal life with God. We get to walk as part of God's counterpart. How cool is that!? There is no cost too high!

Communion

The bread represents Jesus' body broken for us, and the wine/juice represents His blood (bloody sacrifices, remember!) poured out for us. When we "do this in remembrance of Me" we are not only remembering how He died to pay for our sin and reconcile us to God, we are renewing ALL the covenants that God has made with man. Because as Christians we are grafted into Abraham's family, we get the promises of Abraham's covenant, and the blessings of Moses' covenant*! Can we say "Selah"? (stop and think about that for a while!) He is the greater party and we are the weaker in this covenant with Him. We are being reconciled to His heart for us, His counterpart, through the holiness Jesus provided through his death and blood.

* please note that though we do not have to suffer the "curses" of the Mosaic Covenant, we do sometimes end up in "consequences" of sin. These are the natural outcomes of behavior set in place as law, in the same way that gravity is a law set in place by the Creator.

CHAPTER 14
LESSON: THE LORD'S TIMELINE

Topics: Hebrew calendar, the Feasts of the Lord, Jewish Holidays, birthdays, Jesus in the Passover, Discrepancies, 3 days in the grave.

The Hebrew Calendar.

The Jewish calendar is based on the Earth's rotation on its axis, the moon's circling of the Earth, and the Earth's revolution around the sun. But there is no direct correlation among these three phenomena. It takes the moon about 29.5 days to circle the Earth, and the Earth revolves around the sun in about 365¼ days, or about 12.4 lunar months. None of this is divisible into an exact, repeatable pattern year after year. (At least not using any math that mankind has come up with yet).

The Jews have calculated the number of years since Creation by adding up the ages of all the generations of people backward. However, this type of providing a year number, does not prove or disprove that the universe is 5,700 years old, as we understand years. Many Orthodox Jews acknowledge that the first six days of creation are not necessarily 24-hour days. Could a 24-hour day have meaning before the creation of the sun on the fourth day? Dr Gerald Schroeder, a nuclear physicist, authored an interesting article presenting a believable explanation on how God's time is different from our time. Schroeder theorizes that the universe "may be young and old simultaneously" using Einstein's Theory of Relativity to shed light on the Torah's aging of the universe and the age as asserted by modern scientists. [115]

The Hebrew calendar does not provide for weekday names, besides Shabbat, which is the seventh day. They are just called "first day," "second day," etc. A more formal translation would be: "First Day of the Sabbath," etc. [116]

Starting with our "Sunday" (first day) here is how the days are distinguished: Yom Rishon, Yom Sheini, Yom Slishi, Yom R'vi'i', Yom Chamishi, Yom Shishi, Yom Shabbat.

The Hebrew calendar contains the following months:[116]

Hebrew	English	Number	Length	Civil Equivalent
נִיסָן	Nissan	1	30 days	March-April
אִיָּיר	Iyar	2	29 days	April-May
סִיוָן	Sivan	3	30 days	May-June
תַּמּוּז	Tammuz	4	29 days	June-July
אָב	Av	5	30 days	July-August
אֱלוּל	Elul	6	29 days	August-September
תִּשְׁרִי	Tishri	7	30 days	September-October
חֶשְׁוָן	Cheshvan	8	29 or 30 days	October-November
כִּסְלֵו	Kislev	9	30 or 29 days	November-December
טֵבֵת	Tevet	10	29 days	December-January
שְׁבָט	Shevat	11	30 days	January-February
אֲדָר א	Adar I (leap years only)	12	30 days	February-March
אֲדָר אֲדָר ב	Adar (called Adar Beit in leap years)	12 (13 in leap years)	29 days	February-March

Established Feasts of the Lord
Pretty cool, but what does this have to do with us as Christians? Well, Exodus establishes the Feasts of the Lord and when and who celebrates them. God never does away with these feasts. So as Christians, followers

of Jesus the Jewish Messiah, we should also be celebrating these Feasts of the Lord. There are entire books that teach about the Feasts, so we will just touch on these very rich and symbolic yearly events:

Passover (*Pesach*)—an 8-day celebration beginning with a meal to commemorate being set free from slavery in Egypt. Occurs each spring.
First Fruits (*Shavu'ot*)—commemorates the giving of the Torah and the first fruits of the year. Occurs in late spring each year.
Tabernacles (or Harvest or Trumpets) (*Sukkot*)—an 8-day festival commemorating the wandering in the desert. Occurs each fall.

Each of these **Feasts of the Lord** is based on a major event in Jewish History, but did you know that they each have a corresponding event in the Christian world as well? These more current events occurred ON THE VERY DAY OF THESE FEASTS as a fulfillment of the original event which was a foretelling or prophetic event.

Passover/Pesach= Jesus as the Passover Lamb who came to save us out of the slavery of sin if we accept His blood as the payment. Tons and tons more symbolism can be seen within this the feast.

First Fruits=Pentecost. The Holy Spirit filled the men and women in the Upper Room as a first fruit of the many who would be filled throughout the generations and around the world.

Tabernacles=not yet fulfilled. Many believe that Messiah's return will correspond with this Jewish Feast day (i.e. "Harvest").

Of course there are other Jewish holidays:[118] *Purim, Rosh Hashanah, Yom Kippur, Simchat Torah, Tisha b'Av, Hanukkah, Lag b'Omer,* Memorial Day (for soldiers) and Holocaust Remembrance Day, Israel's Independence Day (and a separate day for Jerusalem Day!) Lots of things to celebrate and weep over in the Jewish world. Here is what the holidays remember:

Purim: The Jews being delivered from annihilation by Queen Esther. Began in 474 BC. We retell the story and "boo" Haman, and cheer Mordechai.

Rosh Hashanah: Literally means "the head of the year." The Jewish New Year. We eat apples and dates dipped in honey to signify our hopes for a sweet new year.

Yom Kippur: Holiest day of the year. Known as the Day of Atonement Biblically. The entire nation of Israel shuts down. No working, no driving. It is a day of fasting and prayer for the coming year.

Simchat Torah: celebrates the giving of the Torah on Mount Sinai. We sing and dance in the streets with the Torah.

Tisha b'Av: literally "9th of Av" (Av is a month). The day the spies brought back the bad report after 40 days in the Promised Land (1312 BC). Also it is mourning the day the temple was destroyed in 421 BC *and* 70 AD. First Crusade declared by Pope Urban II in 1095. Many horrible things happen to the Jews, even in exile on this day.[118] The book of Lamentations is read. A day of fasting.

Hanukkah: celebrates the miracle of one day's worth of oil lasting eight days in the Temple until more could be made after Ezra brought back a contingent of Israelites from the 2nd Exile in 139 BC.[117]

Lag b'Omer: The days of Awe. A counting of days that occurs between Passover and *Shavu'ot*. As commanded in Leviticus to count 7 weeks between the physical breaking free of Egypt and the spiritual breaking free when given the Torah. This 33rd day of the 50 days is a holiday. The traditions include bonfires and the mourning observations are lifted, lots of parties and weddings are held this day.

Holocaust Remembrance Day: (*Yom HaShoah*) Israel mourns the loss of 6 million Jews in European nations, murdered by the Nazi party of Germany. One million children. A siren is blown and everyone, including traffic, stops in their tracks for two minutes of standing in observant silence every year.

Memorial Day: (*Yom HaZikaron*) Commemorates the soldiers who have fallen defending Israel. A one-minute siren is blown on the eve of Memorial Day and a two-minute siren is blown on the morning of Memorial Day. Throughout the siren, the complete country comes to a standstill. The public stops working, children stop playing, and drivers stop driving.

Independence Day: (*Yom HaAtzmuat*) Israel declared itself a State, and immediately went to war for 13 months, losing a full 1% of her population.[116]

172

Jerusalem Day: (*Yom Yerushaliam*) celebrates the day the Old City of Jerusalem was unified (liberated from Jordan) to the rest of Israel in 1967 on the 28th Iyar 5727.

Birthdays

One of the neat traditions that Jews have as you probably know is the bar/bat mitzvah. It is calculated according to the birthday of an individual. The child who is turning 13 years old, will be reading/reciting the scripture that week in his or her synagogue. Each Sabbath a particular "Torah Portion" is studied and it is considered prophetic over the week. Kind of like our One Year Bible, the entire Torah (first 5 books) and Haftorah (historic & prophetic books of the Bible) are divided up by a weekly portion to be studied. The week that a person turns 12 or 13 the same portion is read in every synagogue in the world as the week that person was born. It is believed to be prophetic over that person's life and calling.

To find your torah portion, you need to know your birthdate, and time and location are especially important if you were born on a Friday evening, as the weekly portion changes as the Sabbath begins at sundown that day. The website http://www.chabad.org/calendar/birthday.asp can help you calculate your day in the Jewish calendar and will tell you your torah portion. The site: http://bible.ort.org/books/cald5.asp will help you find your Torah and Haftorah portions.

Exercise: Read each portion of Scripture after praying that the Lord will speak to you about what He has spoken over your life by giving you life on a particular date, which He planned before the foundations of the earth! (which is even more meaningful if you already caught the article by Dr Schroeder!)

Jesus in the Passover

Passover is the celebration of the Children of Israel being saved out of Egypt when the angel of death passed over their blood-anointed doors is perhaps the most symbol-rich holiday of the Jewish faith. Christians especially enjoy a whole other level of awe once Jesus' sacrifice of death and his resurrection are observed in this ancient tradition. It is a time specified by God for Jewish children to learn from their parents about their identity and heritage as God's chosen people.

The event that sparked this holiday was the 10th plague of Egypt when Pharaoh finally let the Children of Israel go free. God told Moses to instruct the people (Ex 12) to brush with a hyssop branch the blood of a lamb on the top and sides of their doorframe. It was the blood of a perfect lamb which would save them. Then they were to shut themselves inside and eat the lamb. They were not to come out while the Angel of Death wreaked havoc all over Egypt, killing the firstborn of every creature. Exodus 12:3-11

> Tell the whole community of Israel that on the <u>tenth day of this month [Nissan] each man is to take a lamb for his family</u>, one for each household. If any household is too small for a whole lamb, they must share one with their nearest neighbor, having taken into account the number of people there are. You are to determine the amount of lamb needed in accordance with what each person will eat. The animals you choose must be <u>year-old males without defect</u>, and you may take them from the sheep or the goats. <u>Take care of them until the fourteenth day of the month</u>, when all the people of the community of Israel must <u>slaughter them at twilight</u>. Then they are to take some <u>of the blood and put it on the sides and tops of the doorframes of the houses where they eat the lambs</u>. That same night they are to <u>eat the meat roasted over the fire, along with bitter herbs, and bread made without yeast.</u> Do not eat the meat raw or cooked in water, but roast it over the fire—head, legs and inner parts. Do not leave any of it till morning; if some is left till morning, you must burn it. This is how you are to eat it: with your cloak tucked into your belt, your sandals on your feet and your staff in your hand. Eat it in haste; it is the LORD's Passover. (emphasis mine)

Pharaoh forced Israel to leave without even having time to let their bread rise. However they got to take the bounty of Egypt with them! A few days later of course Pharaoh chased them down with his army, but God parted the Red Sea, allowing His people to cross safely, and then He brought the sea down on Pharaoh and his army, drowning them.

The command to celebrate the Passover (or *Pesach*, pronounced "pay' sock") as a yearly occurrence actually came at the same time as God's instruction on how to survive the passing over. This is the way God set it up: Exodus 12:14-23

> This is a day you are to commemorate; for the generations to come you shall celebrate it as a festival to the Lord—A lasting ordinance. For seven days you are to eat bread made without yeast. On the first day remove the yeast from your houses, for whoever eats anything with yeast in it from the first day through the seventh must be cut off from Israel. On the first day <u>hold a sacred assembly</u>, and another one on the seventh day. <u>Do no work at all on these days</u>, except to prepare food for everyone to eat—that is all you may do. [This underlined description is mine. It will later be known as a "Sabbath"].

> Celebrate the Feast of Unleavened Bread, because it was on this very day that I brought your divisions out of Egypt. Celebrate this day as a lasting ordinance for the generations to come. In the first month you are to eat bread made without yeast, from the evening of the fourteenth day until the evening of the twenty-first day. For seven days no yeast is to be found in your houses. And whoever eats anything with yeast in it must be cut off from the community of Israel, whether he is an alien or native-born. Eat nothing made with yeast. Wherever you live, you must eat unleavened bread."

[This 7-8 days is known as the Feast of the Unleavened Bread, where as the Feast of the Passover, is the actual day that kicks everything off, Nissan 14].

> Then Moses summoned all the elders of Israel and said to them, "Go at once and select the animals for your families and slaughter the Passover lamb. Take a bunch of hyssop, dip it into the blood in the basin and put some of the blood on the top and on both sides of the doorframe. Not one of you shall go out the door of his house until morning. When the LORD goes through the land to strike down the Egyptians, he will see the blood on the top and sides of the doorframe and will

175

pass over that doorway, and he will not permit the destroyer to enter your houses and strike you down.

The following account describes that the Lord is a fulfiller of promises to His people. He did exactly as He said he would both to protect those who covered themselves with the blood of the lamb and to those who sided with Egypt/Pharaoh (Ex 12:29-36).

At midnight the LORD struck down all the firstborn in Egypt, from the firstborn of Pharaoh, who sat on the throne, to the firstborn of the prisoner, who was in the dungeon, and the firstborn of all the livestock as well. Pharaoh and all his officials and all the Egyptians got up during the night, and there was loud wailing in Egypt, for there was not a house without someone dead.

During the night Pharaoh summoned Moses and Aaron and said, "Up! Leave my people, you and the Israelites! Go, worship the LORD as you have requested. Take your flocks and herds, as you have said, and go. And also bless me." The Egyptians urged the people to hurry and leave the country. "For otherwise," they said, "we will all die!" So the people took their dough before the yeast was added, and carried it on their shoulders in kneading troughs wrapped in clothing. The Israelites did as Moses instructed and asked the Egyptians for articles of silver and gold and for clothing. The LORD had made the Egyptians favorably disposed toward the people, and they gave them what they asked for; so they plundered the Egyptians.

The tradition today contains all the original commands, (although, I have not seen too many cloaks tucked in belts during dinner!) but, as in every other culture, a holiday tends to grow. Now a Seder meal can take upwards of three hours. It includes eating a full, sumptuous meal, drinking at least four glasses of wine, eating several herbs as reminders of the bitterness of the slavery that God set them free from, singing both holy and fun songs, and prayers. Because things occur in a particular order, usually a family has a book, or order of service, they follow called a *Haggadah* so that no part is forgotten. (Sample *Haggadah* [119]).

Because of the command to rid the house of all leavening products, modernly, this holiday requires long term preparation. The entire home is cleaned, vacuumed and mopped. Couch cushions, bedding and rugs are beaten to dispose of every crumb which might contain leaven, washing out the cupboards, ovens and refrigerators too. Special dishes are used to avoid any residue of leaven. So the holiday dishes have to be taken out of storage and washed for use. It is a big process. Probably this is where our traditional "spring cleaning" comes from. (Thanks sooo much! To be read with much sarcasm from this author who does not enjoy deep cleaning) Interestingly, even the supermarkets in Israel get rid of all pastas, breads, etc. from their shelves beginning a couple weeks before Passover. Bakeries close down one at a time to clean so people do not have to do without their coffee and pastries, and the coffee shops reopen having changed their products to carry only non-leavened pastries and kosher-for-Passover coffee, which do not taste as bad as they sound. Pizzerias just close for the eight day holiday.

Seder Plate: "Seder" is the proper name for the Passover meal that takes place on the first day of the week-long holiday. The centerpiece of the modern Seder table is a special plate that contains elements to be consumed by those observing the feast.

1. Hyssop—modernly parsley is used—represents the hyssop branches used to apply the blood of the lamb to the doorways. It is also a reminder of the hyssop used by the High Priest to sprinkle blood on the altar.
2. Salt Water—represents the tears of the Children of Israel and the parting of the Red Sea. The parsley is dipped into the cup of salt water and eaten.
3. Bitter Herbs—modernly horseradish is used—represents the bitterness of slavery in Egypt. (For Christians, also the betrayal of Judas from John 13)
4. *Charosef* (sweet mixture of walnuts, cinnamon, and apple chunks)—represents mortar as used to hold bricks together. It signifies that the promises of God (deliverance) are sweet in our mouths. The Children of Israel were delivered after 400 years of slavery.
5. Hardboiled Egg—represents life, or the lamb. The roasted sacrifice.

6. Shank bone—represents the sacrificial lamb. Also, since the Roman conquering in 70 AD, it reminds us that there is no temple in Jerusalem. Reminds Christians that Jesus is our sacrificial Lamb.
7. Matzah bread—bread made without yeast—represents the quick getaway that God provided for His people. They did not have time for the bread to rise. Three "slices" of Matzah (matzot is plural form) are separated from the rest and are placed into a Matzah cover or envelope. The middle one is taken out during the course of the *Haggadah* and broken in half. Half is placed back in the middle and the other half is hidden away for the children to find later. Considered a "dessert" as a last element of the Passover meal. The hidden half is called the *Afikomen*. To the Jews it represents the broken Passover lamb. Here is another explanation:

> "...some Jews suggest there is a deeper purpose, namely to show the mysterious order of the universe, waiting to be uncovered. According to this perspective, the children seek to find the Afikomen because they represent all of us as children in the search for the unknown... Once the Afikomen is redeemed, it is immediately broken into pieces and eaten by every celebrant. It is to be eaten while reclining on the left side, promptly without interruption, and according to halachic sayings, before midnight."[120]

The Four cups of wine are drunk throughout the meal at different times as designated by the *Haggadah*. They represent the following in order of being drunk: 1. Sanctification 2. Judgment 3. Redemption 4. Praise. A fifth cup of wine is poured for Elijah. It is left un-drunk. Here is the explanation in Rabbi Barry Dov Lerner's words

> The cup of Elijah derives from a problem in Talmudic Law. The problem is not knowing exactly how many cups of wine to drink at the Seder, four or five. The number of cups is based on the four expressions of deliverance, but there is actually a fifth expression of deliverance. So, the rabbis came up with the perfect Jewish compromise. We fill the fifth cup, but we don't drink from it. And since Elijah will [precede] the

Messiah, who will be able to tell us whether four or five cups are correct, we make the fifth cup of wine Elijah's cup.

In some Seder services, each person at the Seder contributes some wine to the fifth cup, symbolizing everyone sharing in the messianic hope. At other Seder services, wine from the cup of Elijah is mixed with the fourth cup.[121]

At some point during the meal the youngest child in attendance goes to open the door and look for Elijah, as it is believed that one day he will show up as the Messiah at this feast. So there is always a place set for him, a chair and place setting that is left empty at the table. The child also asks the important question that gets things rolling, "Why is tonight different from all other nights?"

Formerly, for 1200 years, when the lamb was taken into the home for the four days, the father was carefully inspecting it for any imperfection, while the children were enjoying keeping it as a pet and becoming attached emotionally to it.

Pesach Foods: These days, there is not much lamb slaughtering done. While lamb is a common dish at a Passover Seder, any type of kosher meat can be found on the Seder table, roasted chicken or turkey, beef brisket, fish, and depending on the size of the crowd, maybe all of the above. Among Ashkenazi Jews, gefilte fish and matzah ball soup are traditionally eaten at the beginning of the meal. Any dish or vegetable combination as long as it does not contain leaven (corn does) can be found on a Seder table. Most packaged items, even potato chips, come with a special label stating that they are "kosher for Passover."

The Christian view spelled out .

The Lamb—The blood of a sacrificial lamb saving the Jews is a fore-picture of Jesus as Messiah. When He arrived in Jerusalem, Jesus made what the scriptures call His triumphal entry. This day was the 10th of Nissan, based on John 12:1 and 12:12. Elsewhere in the city, probably on the Temple Mount, it was Lamb-Selection Day, the day Jewish fathers chose the lamb for their families and presented them to the priests for divine approval (Ex 12:3) before taking them home for the next four days. These are the requirements for the lamb as recorded in Exodus 12:4 included with Jesus' qualification:

- a lamb without blemish, must be perfect. Jesus never sinned
- a male. Jesus was male.
- a lamb of less than one year old, typifying innocence. Again, Jesus never sinned.
- separated from the goats, set apart for a special purpose. Jesus was holy and set apart by God in everything He did.
- no bones could be broken – prophecies that the Messiah would not have broken bones. Jesus, even as cruel a death as He suffered, not one bone was broken.
- the blood of the lamb was to be spilled. Jesus spilled His blood both in the beating and from the nails and spear piercings.
- the lamb must be roasted with fire. Jesus experienced the searing pain of our sin.
- deliverance is for everyone who is covered by the blood of the lamb.

Truly Jesus symbolized and fulfilled all the anticipations contained in the traditions of Moses. He was the Lamb of God who laid down His life so that His blood could bring deliverance to all who accept His sacrifice.

Jesus was chosen by the people's worship, singing "Hosanna," waving palm branches, and throwing down their cloaks on Lamb-Selection Day (celebrated as Palm Sunday). On the 14th of Nissan, Pontias Pilate, the ruler of Jerusalem at that time (think of him in the role of the family father), examined Jesus and found Him to be without cause for blame (innocent) and he washed his hands of the man and the religious community of Jews who wanted Him dead. Incidentally, hand washing is also part of the Passover tradition in the *Haggadah* as well.

In Matthew's Gospel he describes it this way (Matt 27:24-25)
> When Pilate saw that he was getting nowhere, but that instead an uproar was starting, he took water and washed his hands in front of the crowd. "I am innocent of this man's blood," he said. "It is your responsibility!" All the people answered, "Let his blood be on us and on our children!"

John 19:4 & 13-14 Once more Pilate came out and said to the Jews, "Look, I am bringing him out to you to let you know that I find no basis for a charge against him..." When Pilate heard this, he brought Jesus out and sat down on the judge's seat at a place known as the Stone Pavement (which in Aramaic is Gabbatha). It was the day of Preparation of Passover Week, about the sixth hour. "Here is your king," Pilate said to the Jews.

Thus Jesus is found worthy to represent the Jews by the ruling authority, in the same way the High Priest was declaring lambs worthy to represent a family. Both Jesus and the lamb would die and the blood would cover the sins of the people they represent.

Another interesting little historical tidbit according to Richard Deem's article *How the Passover reveals Jesus Christ.*[122]

The people did not understand the significance of this, (their worship) since they greeted Him with palm branches and hailed Him as King, shouting "Hosanna," which means "save us." However, they were not looking for a spiritual Savior, but a political savior. Palm branches were a symbol of freedom and defiance...Jesus' reaction was to weep, since He realized that they did not understand the Messiah's purpose in coming.

At the Last Supper, it was the Passover meal. The last cup of wine Jesus drank was the third cup. If you recall, it was called the Cup of Redemption. It was the one He held up and said, "This is my blood." The last bread He ate would have been the Afikomen, representative of Himself. He said, "This is my body." Remember the three pieces of matzah that are separated from the rest on the table and tucked into a little cloth envelope? For Christians these three represent the Trinity: Father, Son and Holy Spirit. The middle piece (Jesus) is separated from the other two and broken in half. Symbolizing the Son's broken body and separation from the Godhead. The Afikomen is hidden away like when Jesus was hidden away in the grave. Then at the end of the meal the Afikomen is searched for and found. And the child that finds it, receives a prize from his or her father! Just like when we find Jesus.

181

Even the matzah itself, exclusive of its central place on the table and in the ceremony, is representative of Jesus' suffering. The matzah contains no yeast or puffiness. That the yeast represents religious pride is Jesus' own definition (Matt 16:5-12). Jesus contains no pride or arrogance. The matzah is striped, pierced and scorched bread, as was Jesus.

1. Jesus called himself the Bread of Life (John 6:33-51).
2. He was pierced with nails and a spear and he bore the stripes of the whip.
   a. This was prophesied in
      Ps 22:16: Dogs have surrounded me; a band of evil men has encircled me, they have pierced my hands and my feet.
      Isaiah 53:5 But he was pierced for our transgressions, he was crushed for our iniquities; the punishment that brought us peace was upon him, and by his wounds we are healed.
      Zech 12:10 They will look on me, the one they have pierced, and they will mourn for him as one mourns for an only child
   b. This was fulfilled when Jesus was pierced by nails and with a spear
      John 19:33-34 But when they came to Jesus and found that he was already dead, they did not break his legs. Instead, one of the soldiers pierced Jesus' side with a spear, bringing a sudden flow of blood and water

The scorching was more allegorical, I think, representative of the scorching of our sins heaped upon Him. Though perhaps it is related to the flames of hell, where Jesus went to grab the keys of death, hell and the grave while He was physically dead and in the grave here on earth.

> Revelation 1:18 I am the Living One; I was dead, and behold I am alive for ever and ever! And I hold the keys of death and Hades.

And all of these symbols (Matzah, Afikomen, the envelope, cups of wine, the Seder plate) are repeated year after year as a Passover tradition. The original Passover event itself was a symbol, a foretelling, of the coming Passover Lamb, Messiah Jesus. It was practiced for 1,200 years before Jesus and now, nearly 2,000 years since Passover has been fulfilled, and those signs are annually before God's people.

Remember the child that went to the door to look for Elijah? Well, He did show up at Passover, just as the Jews suspected, unfortunately, the Messiah did not fit the description they were hoping for: a king who would come in and right the world (wipe out the Romans) in their favor. Instead He came as a humble servant who tried to right individual hearts with their Father God.

Time of Death Significance

During Passover, the lambs were slaughtered and died at "twilight" (Ex 12:6). The evening prayers and the slaughter of the Passover lambs would have begun about 3-4 PM in the temple in Jerusalem based on the time of year and when sunset falls during the month of *Nissan* (after seeing this information from various sources, I verified it (on Feb 23, 2010 from www.timeanddate.com) according to the timeline of Jesus' crucifixion, though Jesus was fixed to the cross earlier in the day, it is very clear in the Gospels that Jesus died at the ninth hour (Matt 27:47, Mark 15:34, and Luke 23:44). Because of the ancient tradition to start counting the day's hours at sunup (approximately 6 to 6:30 AM) count nine hours forward of 6 AM to arrive at 3 PM. Jesus was the perfect lamb, chosen by the people in worship on Nisan 10, and declared "without blemish" by the authority of the day was sacrificed at the **exact time** that the lambs were being sacrificed in the temple, just on the other side of the city wall.

> For the previous 1,200 years, the priest would blow the shophar (ram's horn) at 3:00 p.m. - the moment the lamb was sacrificed, and all the people would pause to contemplate the sacrifice for sins on behalf of the people of Israel. On Good Friday at 3:00, when Jesus was being crucified, He said, "It is finished"- at the moment that the Passover lamb was sacrificed and the shophar was blown from the Temple"[122]

An added bit of symbolism shows up in the original Passover event. Seven days after the Israelites experienced the first Passover in Egypt, they came to the Red Sea and went through it. The Israelites crossing the Red Sea can be compared to Christian baptism. A passing from the death of slavery to the life led by God, even through the desert wilderness into the Promised Land of heaven. Interesting that when the 40 years of wandering were up, God led Israel through another body of water (Jordan River) to take them into their new lives in the Promised Land.

The Discrepancies: If you have not yet stumbled across the discrepancies that have challenged many Biblical scholars, here they are:

1. How could Jesus have celebrated the Passover as Scripture says He did with His disciples on one night, and the next day be the Passover Lamb killed to atone for the sin of the world, as Scripture clearly states that He did?

2. How did Jesus rise from the dead after 3 days when clearly Good Friday night to Sunday morning is only 2 nights and a day, no matter how you do the math?

We will start with the Passover Lamb issue. John MacArther[123] explained the situation and traditions in a way that I could finally grasp. It is all about timing. I will summarize for you.

Matthew 26:17-21 describes that the disciples made preparations for the meal, and that their lamb was killed in the afternoon and they ate and celebrated together, and then walked to the Garden of Gethsemane minus Judas Iscariot who went to the religious leaders to betray Jesus to them. Jesus was then captured by soldiers, held overnight at Caiaphas's house, and brought to "trail" in the morning. John 18:28 says "Jewish leaders took Jesus from Caiaphas to the palace of the Roman governor. By now it was early morning and to avoid ceremonial uncleanness they did not enter the palace, because they wanted to be able to eat the Passover."

So how did Jesus eat his Passover one night and the religious leaders eat theirs the next night? It was not a "private Passover" because the lambs could only be slain at a particular time.

> We know it (Jesus' Passover meal) wasn't just another meal because Jesus insisted that it be eaten inside the city of Jerusalem. They constantly referred to it as the Passover... They sang a hymn when they were finished with the meal, which was true of the Passover. And when Judas left, the disciples thought that he was going to give money to the poor, which was a typical thing to do at the Passover.[121]

This mystery can be understood based on how a day was calculated. We Westerners "reckon" a day from midnight to midnight. Jews today reckon a day from sun down to sun down. But that was not always the case. They had two options. They could also reckon from sunrise to sunrise. Normally, that is how they did it and how they counted hours (i.e. "in the ninth hour"), with only the Sabbath and certain festival days as prescribed by the Torah being reckoned from sunset to sunset. For example Exodus 12:18: the Feast of Unleavened Bread is to be celebrated from sunset to sunset on Nisan 14 to Nisan 21.

Perhaps this reckoning came to be as from Genesis 1:5 when God says "the evening and morning were the first day" and so forth. Although our calendars reflect a midnight to midnight reckoning, we think of the day beginning when we rise in the morning. So did they. Matthew 28:1 is a prime example. "In the end of the Sabbath . . . it began to dawn toward the first day of the week." The first day of the week began at dawn.

> Regarding the Passover we can see a sunrise to sunrise reckoning in Deuteronomy 16:4. Combining that with Exodus 12:18, the Passover day could be calculated from sunset to sunset or sunrise to sunrise. Josephus, who was a Pharisee living in Jesus' day, explained that the law of the Passover called for the Paschal lamb to be eaten during the night with nothing left for morning (Antiquities, iii. 10. 5). The Talmud, the codification of Jewish law, says it had to be eaten by midnight, which seems to indicate that the new day began after sunset (Pesahim x. 9, Zebahim v. 8).[123]

History seems to point to the Galileans and Pharisees reckoning their days from sunrise to sunrise, and Judeans and Sadducees reckoning from sunset to sunset. The latter were the ruling body in Jerusalem. From the Talmud (Pesahim iv. 5), Galileans would not work on the day of Passover because their day began at sunrise. The Judeans would work until midday because their Passover Day began at sunset.

> Matthew 26:17 follows the Galilean reckoning, so Jesus and the disciples had to kill their lamb on Thursday and eat the Passover meal Thursday evening. The Judeans and Sadducees didn't begin their Passover day festivities until late on Thursday and wouldn't kill their

lambs until the prescribed time of day on Friday. That brings harmony among John 18:28 and the other gospels.[123]

It is so like God to arrange into the timekeeping of history at this time a way for Jesus to both keep the Passover (on Thursday) to transform it into the Lord's Supper, Communion etc, and also die between 3:00 and 5:00 o'clock to BE the Passover Lamb on Friday during the Judean Passover day. And the priests didn't put up a fuss probably because it helped spread their workload of slaughtering the Passover lambs of millions of Jews gathered in Jerusalem as prescribed into two days.

Two days of Passover was not problematic for Jews of the day, nor the writers of the New Testament; no one even mentioned it; it was normal. A correlation with an American holiday that is split in its celebration can be found in Christmas. Do you open your presents and celebrate on Christmas Eve after the sun has set or must you wait until Christmas morning? Either way, it is still Christmas.

The Friday-to-Sunday is 3 days discrepancy.
Quick question: if you got off work at 3:00 in the afternoon on a Friday and had to show up for work again on Sunday morning, would you call it a three-day weekend? I think not. So let's dispense with the "any part of a day was counted as a full day" argument. For me, it just doesn't hold water.

The discrepancy between the prophecies of three full days in the grave versus the Friday night to Sunday morning scenario, stems from traditions of men and one small translation error. That Jesus was to have been dead three days is unchallenged. That is everywhere in scripture, both in Old Testament prophecy and in New Testament accounts. The tradition of men, namely the Catholic Church, cites that Good Friday is the day Jesus died, based on these scriptures Mark 15:42, Luke 23:54, John 19:14, 31, & 42. The phrase used is Jesus was buried "the day before the Sabbath."

As the Jewish weekly Sabbath came on Saturday, scholars have assumed Jesus was crucified on Good Friday. This is poor reasoning because the Bible bears abundant testimony that the Jews had other annual

186

Sabbaths beside the weekly Sabbath which fell each
Friday evening to Saturday evening.[122]

The "Sabbath" as it is described in Leviticus 23:3, is indicative of a day
of rest and of sacred assembly. It is not as we suppose: just another name
for "Saturday." Think of it more as meaning "Holy Day." The Jews were
commanded to observe a Holy Day once a week. But the Lord also
commanded other Holy Days when He required that there be a sacred
assembly and no work done. Other prescribed Sabbaths included in the
Leviticus 23 description of holidays/feasts are as follows:

1. 14th and 15th day of the first month—Lev 23:6 (Passover) (and
   the last day of the feast as well)
2. 1st day of the seventh month—Lev 23:23 (Feast of Trumpets)
3. 10th day of the seventh month—Lev 23:27-28 (Day of
   Atonement)
4. 15th day of the seventh month—Lev 23:34 (Feast of Tabernacles)
5. 15th day +8 days of the seventh month—Lev 23: 36 (end of the
   Feast of Tabernacles)

Lev 23:32 is a description of Sabbath meaning a holy day rather than just
another name for the 7th day. "It is a Sabbath of rest for you, and you
must deny yourselves. From the evening of the ninth day of the month
until the following evening you are to observe your Sabbath."

It is the translation of the word "Sabbath" in Matthew 28:1 that has
caused so much confusion. In the original Greek, this "Sabbath" is
actually plural in number. So it should be read, "After the Sabbaths, at
dawn on the first day of the week, Mary Magdalene and the other Mary
went to look at the tomb." It is the Friday-to-Sunday tradition of man that
has caused translators to misinterpret this word. "This (corrected
translation) allows for an annual Sabbath on Thursday and a regular
Sabbath on Saturday."[124] The only question this interpretation leaves me
with is this: Why didn't the women go to anoint Jesus' body on the day
after Passover was completed, which was not a holy day, but preparation
day for the weekly Shabbat?

So the following pages are a timeline chart that tries to untangle the three
full days in the grave:

Nisan 9	Nisan 10	Nisan 11	Nisan 12	Nisan 13

Sunset · Midnight · Sunrise · Sunset · Midnight · Sunrise · Noon · Sunset · Midnight · Sunrise · Noon · Sunset · Midnight · Sunrise · Noon · Sunset · Midnight · Sunrise · Noon

Jesus arrived at Bethany. Feet anointed by Mary. Jn. 12:1-7

Jesus triumphantly enters Jerusalem. Jn 12:12-13

Lamb selection Ex. 12:3

Jesus weeps over Jerusalem. Lk 19:41:44

Jesus curses Fig tree Mk 11:12-14.

Jesus cleanses temple of money-changers. Mk. 11:15-18

Sadducees question Him. Mt 22:23

Jesus goes to Mt of Olives at night after teaching in Temple. Lk 21:37-38

Fig tree found withered. Mk 11:20

Priests, scribes & elders challenge Jesus' authority. Mk 11:27-28

Judas seeks to betray Jesus. Mt 26:14

Jesus tells disciples where to prepare Passover. Lk 22:7-13

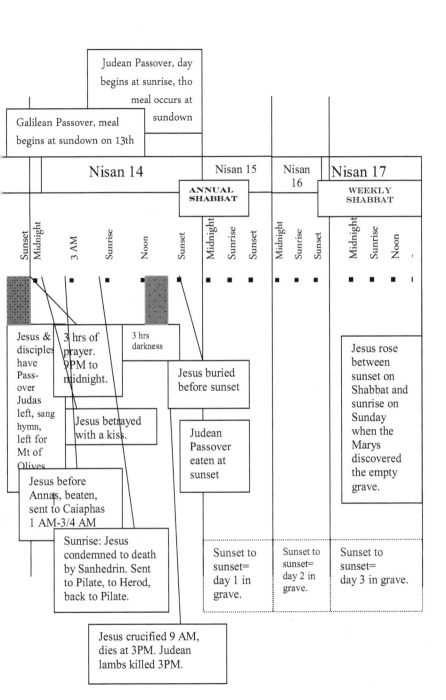

Judean Passover, day begins at sunrise, tho meal occurs at sundown

Galilean Passover, meal begins at sundown on 13th

Nisan 14

Nisan 15

ANNUAL SHABBAT

Nisan 16

Nisan 17

WEEKLY SHABBAT

Sunset | Midnight | 3 AM | Sunrise | Noon | Sunset | Midnight | Sunrise | Sunset | Midnight | Sunrise | Sunset | Midnight | Sunrise | Noon

Jesus & disciples have Passover Judas left, sang hymn, left for Mt of Olives.

3 hrs of prayer. 9PM to midnight.

3 hrs darkness

Jesus betrayed with a kiss.

Jesus buried before sunset

Judean Passover eaten at sunset

Jesus rose between sunset on Shabbat and sunrise on Sunday when the Marys discovered the empty grave.

Jesus before Annas, beaten, sent to Caiaphas 1 AM-3/4 AM

Sunrise: Jesus condemned to death by Sanhedrin. Sent to Pilate, to Herod, back to Pilate.

Sunset to sunset= day 1 in grave.

Sunset to sunset= day 2 in grave.

Sunset to sunset= day 3 in grave.

Jesus crucified 9 AM, dies at 3PM. Judean lambs killed 3PM.

CHAPTER 15
LESSON: THE HEBREW LANGUAGE
Topics: history, revival of language, Ben Yahuda's story, letters chart, Examples. Intercession for Israel

The Promise
Zephaniah 3:9
Then I will restore to the peoples of pure language that they all may call on the name of the Lord, to serve Him with one accord.

History
According to Genesis 2:16, God *spoke* to Adam (incidentally it was instruction concerning the two trees of the Garden). How did God speak lest He used language? And according to Genesis 11:1, the whole earth spoke one language (presumably, the same language God first used to speak to Adam when He created him) until God confused their languages at the Tower of Babel. The confusion of languages is recorded in Gen 11:9). Up to this point all recorded names are Hebrew. This means only that every name has a meaning in the Hebrew language.
A few examples:
1. "Cain" sounds like the Hebrew word for *I have given birth.* (Seth was the first human born of a human).
2. "Seth" sounds like the Hebrew word *to give.* (When Eve bore Seth, she said, "God has given me another child to take the place of Abel." Gen 4: 25-26).
3. "Methuselah" sounds like the Hebrew words for *his death brings.* (In the year that Methuselah died, the great Flood occurred).[125]
4. "Peleg" sounds like the Hebrew word for *divided.* (During his lifetime the earth divided. Think Continental Shift as you probably studied in World History).

It is not until the time of Noah's great grandchildren is there a name recorded with origins outside the Hebrew language, such as *Nimrod.* (Ham-Cush-Nimrod as recorded in Genesis 10:8). Nimrod's generation was the same timeframe as when the Tower of Babel and dispersion of languages occurred. (Shem-Arphaxed-Eber-Peleg as recorded in Genesis 10:21-25).

Both Jewish tradition and many Christian scholars believe that the original language that God used was Hebrew.

Revival

Hebrew is the ONLY language to be revived after any significant period of time that a language has fallen into disuse. Of course Hebrew has been used throughout the ages by Jews to recite the Torah and prayers, but only "holy words" were kept in use. Eliezer ben Yahuda is credited as the Father of the Modern Hebrew language. It was through his relentless research to "find" words, and his unbending accuracy at creating new words which could not have existed in ancient Hebrew (such as "airplane") that modern Hebrew is full of integrity as a language.

Ben Yahuda's story: a great longer version can be found in *Tongues of the Prophets: The Life Story of Eliezer Ben Yahuda,* written by Robert St. John.

Ben Yahuda was born in 1858 in Lithuania to an Orthodox Jewish family called Perlman. He changed his name when, like Jacob to Israel, he received a revelation of his life's calling at age 17. He was studying in a Yeshiva with a free-thinking rabbi when all this occurred.

> "It was as if the heavens had suddenly opened, and a clear incandescent light flashed before my eyes, and a mighty inner voice sounded in my ears: the renascence of Israel on its ancestral soil." This vision remained with him, as he wrote, "the more the nationalist concept grew in me, the more I realized what a common language is to a nation..." Thus he dedicated himself to this goal: 'Yisrael be'artzo uvilshono' the rebirth of the nation of Israel in its own land, speaking its own language.[126]

Of course ben Yahuda was not the first one to think of a new Israel, but he was the one with the God-given calling to revive the language, and keep it true to its origins. And it was a lot of work, and expensive too.

In 1881, ben Yahuda migrated to Israel, picking up a wife, Deborah Jonas, on the way, in Vienna. They established the first Hebrew-only home in Jerusalem (the area was still called Palestine). When people came to visit, they were allowed only to speak Hebrew. Eliezer was so committed to his cause that the ben Yahudas would arrange for a translator to be present or take guests away from their home if they could not speak Hebrew (even though the ben Yahudas understood them just fine). His wife was a little more hesitant than he was, but she agreed to the experiment and Ben-Zion, their son, became the first child in two millennia to be raised with Hebrew as his native language!!!

According to the Jewish Agency for Israel,

> Soon after his arrival in Jerusalem, Ben-Yehuda accepted a teaching position at the Alliance School which became the first school where some courses were taught in Hebrew, due to Eliezer's insistence that Hebrew be the official language of instruction for Jewish subjects. Ben-Yehuda wrote for "Hakhavatzelet" (The Lily), a Hebrew literary periodical, and launched "Hatzvi" -- The Deer -- a weekly newspaper. "Hatzvi" was the first Hebrew paper to report what was happening throughout the land. For this paper Eliezer needed to coin new Hebrew words for objects and verbs that did not exist in the days of the last Hebrew commonwealth.

> Ben-Yehuda's wife, Deborah, died of tuberculosis in 1891. Six months later, her younger sister offered to marry Ben-Yehuda and care for Deborah's two small children. An emancipated woman of great drive and conviction, she made it her life's work to support Eliezer and his enterprise. Adopting the Hebrew name Hemdah, she learned Hebrew fluently in record time, became a reporter for his paper, and in time took over as editor, in order to allow Eliezer to concentrate on his research of the lost Hebrew words that the reborn tongue required.

> It was in response to his article in "The Dawn" that the first group of halutzim (pioneers), the BILU group, came to settle on the land.[127]

Ben Yahuda wrote text books in Hebrew and got them into teacher's hands. He suffered much at the hands and words of the Orthodox Jews living in Jerusalem at the time. He was even excommunicated and suffered persecution because of his political agenda. Unfortunately, he harbored those feeling of resentment toward the religious orthodox community most of his life. He wrote, published and delivered or mailed two Hebrew-only newspapers. He spent most of his life working, usually

18 hours a day, on a Hebrew dictionary entitled *Complete Dictionary of Ancient and Modern Hebrew*. The first volume was published in 1910. He wrote and had published volumes 1-6 himself through funding from Baron Rothschild, a benefactor in France. Ben Yahuda's son, Ehud, continued on in this work that ended up being 17 volumes long. "In December 1922, ben Yehuda, 64, died of tuberculosis, from which he suffered most of his life. He was buried on the Mount of Olives in Jerusalem. His funeral was attended by 30,000 people."[127] He also lost his first wife and several children to this disease.

Now the main touristy shopping drag in Jerusalem is named after him: Ben Yahuda Street. Most Israeli cities have a street named after him too. Hebrew is offered in a five-month intensive study for new immigrants for free and for foreigners at a low cost. It is called *Ulpan*, and there are several different varieties of learning styles to choose from.

Hebrew Letters in order from right to left as they are read:
Every letter has its own meaning and its own numerical value. Several of the letters are different in their shape and name if they fall at the end of a word. For example: the N letter *nun* (sounds like the English word "noon") becomes a *nunsofit* (Pronounced: "noon' so feet") if it is the last letter in a word, and it has a longer "tail." There are no lowercase and upper case letters as in English, but the block letters or print letters can look as dissimilar to hand written letters as English's print letters are to cursive writing.

Alef	א	A Vowel sounds
Bet	ב/ב	B/V
Gimmel	ג	G
Dalet	ד	D
Hey	ה	H
Vav	ו	V or vowel sound

Zayin	ז	Z
Chet	ח	Ch/ guteral
Tet	ט	T
Yod	י	Y / I vowel sounds
Kof kofsofit	כּ/כ ך	K or ch
Lamed	ל	L
Mem memsofit	מ ם	M, soft m
Nun nunsofit	נ ן	N, soft n
Samech	ס	S
Ayin	ע	Vowel sounds, other
Pey peysofit	פּ/פ ף	P/f
Tsadi Tsadisofit	צ ץ	Ts/Z
Kuf	ק	Q/K
Resh	ר	R
Shen	שׁ/שׂ	S/ Sh
Tav	ת	T

Interesting Hebrew idiosyncrasies:

The Hebrew language is made up of just 22 consonants and 3 vowel place holders (they don't really have sounds on their own, unlike English vowels). There are seven basic "branches" or "forms" that any word in Hebrew can be fitted into. Based on which form the word is in, it changes its definition, but in the root, it is related to all the other definitions. Think of it like a menorah. The forms are the consonant sounds in a fixed pattern that are represented by each branch, but the root (stem of the Menorah) remains the same. The root is called the "shoresh" and is usually formed of 3-4 Hebrew letters.

(Photo taken in the "upper room" Nov. 2009, by Kim Frolander)

Example:

The root letters Mim, dalet, bet, resh, can have "vowel sounds" added to form Hebrew words such as *Midbar* or *Medaber*. But there is always a connection in the meaning and it LOOKS like the same word in Hebrew (Mim, dalet, bet, resh). At the risk of sounding like a conspiracy theorist, it is as if God imbedded a code for us to unwind and meditate on. Almost a divine puzzle to figure out WHY God relates some words with each other. What does He reveal about Himself in the language of our example word?

Well, translating our example words above, *Midbar* means "desert." And *Medaber* is a present tense verb "speaking." Could God be saying that when people are in the desert He is speaking? I don't think it is too big a stretch, and doesn't it make the idea of "the desert season" so much more tolerable to know that God will speak to us when we are in the desert, perhaps even that He has brought us into that desert season in order to speak to us?

The word *Amen*

Here is an interesting tidbit most English-speaking people miss. "Our" English word *amen*, is actually Hebrew. The shoresh (root) is spelled lamed, hey, mem, nunsofit. When an alef is added, (lamed, hey, alef, mem, nunsofit) if forms the word Lehamin. Which is an infinitive verb "to believe".

To change the verb to present tense the beginning is changed (similar to how English endings are changed: i.e. work, working, worked). Present tense of this verb is *Ma'amin* (Believing).

When making this verb past tense it is fascinating. The Hebrew past tense for "he (or it) believed" is pronounced "amen."

So every time you end your prayer with "amen" you are announcing that you already believed. May we pray with such conviction that our belief is a sure and done thing!

Star of David, *Magen David*—as found on the Israeli flag.
"Magen" actually means shield, not star. One explanation of its origin is from when King David would hang his two triangular-shaped shields, one on top of each other. It formed the shape of a star. Interestingly, the Hebrew word for ambulance comes from the infinitive of "to protect" so it is extremely symbolic being that the shield or star of David is on the ambulance and flags, as it is related to protecting.[128]

David (Dalit, Vav, Dalit)
This combination in a shoresh with different vowel sounds added can be the word *dod* (dalit, yod, dalit) meaning "beloved." Or *dud* meaning "jar" which is a vessel. But when the middle letter is used as a consonant, it is a vav and forms the word/name *David*. This spelling provides an underlying connection between David and vessel. Is it a coincidence then that the first recorded David in the Bible is a "vessel of worship" and beloved of God, described as a "man after God's own heart"? I think not. It was described in his name.[128]

If this study of the language excites you, look for more awesome word studies in Joel Hoffman's book, *In the Beginning: A short History of the Hebrew Language*. He extrapolates the names of God and implications of when God changes people's names (Abram and Sarai).[129]

Intercession for Israel.

Pray for the peace of Jerusalem, as David says in Psalms 122:6-9.

> Pray for the peace of Jerusalem:
> "May those who love you be secure.
>
> May there be peace within your walls
> and security within your citadels."
>
> For the sake of my brothers and friends,
> I will say, "Peace be within you."
>
> For the sake of the house of the LORD our God,
> I will seek your prosperity.

But how do we go about that more specifically? Most importantly, ask the Holy Spirit to lead you in the prayers He wants prayed over the Lord's Land at any particular moment. Things are in flux in Israel on an hour by hour basis. But here are some ideas to get you rolling:

1. secure borders, and alert patrols and airport screeners
2. that leadership in Israel's government would be godly, wise and courageous
3. IDF, lone soldiers, young soldiers, wisdom and strategic planning by leaders
4. that world leadership would have their eyes and ears opened by God to the truth of what goes on between Israel and the Arab world
5. Police and special units to have protection, discernment and wisdom
6. Arab Christians and Arab pre-Christians in the Land
7. Messianic Believers for strength, wisdom, courage, and divine encounters that will keep the Gospel message going forth without being watered down
8. Israeli economy, finances of individuals, and the viability of the Shekel in the world market
9. Jewish rabbis to have dynamic encounters with God & share those with their congregations

10. Christian Ministries in Israel, that the leadership is refreshed. For them to be passing the baton strategically, clear thinking and planning, finances, that the pressures they face on a daily basis in the spirit and from the government and being in ministry would roll off their backs.
11. Volunteers in the Land, for energy, finances, courage, an ease in transition, frustrations of culture clashes would be simply resolved
12. Revival: Secular Jews who no longer believe in the God of the Bible and miracles would have heart changes and be turned back to Him. That they would realize who they are
13. Jews from afar would respond to the Lord's whistle and make *aliyah* in His timing for their families.
14. New immigrants would be provided for and new jobs would be created
15. Settlers in the non-citified areas would be safe and be strategic in planning their new cities
16. That God would frustrate the plans of the enemy and sew confusion in the enemy's camp that no evil thing would befall Israel or her people.

Write in some prayers the Lord gives you for His special People

SOURCES

Introduction

1.1 Rabbi Jamie Cowan live in the "Jewish History Conference" at Richmond International House of Prayer, Richmond, Virginia, March 2011.

1. *Fiddler on the Roof.* Mirisch - Cartier Production Film. 1971.
2. Rich, Tracey R. 2006 (5766*). Judaism 101*. Retrieved Dec 9, 2009, from http://www.jewfaq.org/prayer/tallit.htm

Chapter 1

3. Ancient Jewish Diaspora Archive. (n.d.). Retrieved Dec 8, 2009 from http://diaspora.commons.yale.edu/index.php?option=com_content&task=view&id=16&Itemid=42.
4. Map is mine, adapted from SpiritRestoration.org. (n.d.). Retrieved Dec 8, 2009 from: http://spiritrestoration.org/Church/Research%20History%20and%20Great%20Links/Maps/Jewish%20Diaspora.gif
5. SimpleToRemember.Com. (n.d.). Retrieved Dec 10, 2009 from http://www.simpletoremember.com/articles/a/History JewishPersecution/
6. SpiritRestoration.org. (n.d.). Retrieved Dec 10, 2009 from http://spiritrestoration.org/Church/Research%20History%20and%20Great%20Links/timleine_of_the_old_testament_chart.htm
7. Hirsch, Emil G., and McCurdy, J, Frederic. 2002. Retrieved 11 Dec, 2009 from http://www.jewishencyclopedia.com/view.jsp?artid=295&letter=I&search=hebrews#838.
8. Ministry of Foreign Affairs, Israel. 2008. Retrieved Dec 11, 2009 from http://www.mfa.gov.il/MFA/MFAArchive/2000_2009/2002/10/Aliyah)

Chapter 2

9. NIV Study Bible. 1985. Zondervan House Publishers, Grand Rapids, MI.

Chapter 3

10. Reich, Bernard. 2005. *A Brief History of Israel*. Facts on file publishing. New York.
11. InTheDoghouse. (n.d.) Retrieved Jan 11, 2010 from http://hubpages.com/hub/Ten-Plagues-For-Ten-Gods.
12. Photos credited to Wyatt, Ron. 1998. By WyattMuseum.com. Retrieved June 6, 2011 from http://www.wyattmuseum.com/red-sea-crossing-04.htm.

13. 12 Johnson, Paul. 2005. *A History of the Jews.* 2nd Ed. Harper Perennial Publishers. New York, New York. p.26).
14. An explanation of the calf can be found at http://www.holocaustrevealed.org/English/S/p222.html

Chapter 4
15. Approximate date as listed at www.ohr.edu. Retrieved January 27, 2010.
16. Samuel's birth year according to (http://spiritrestoration.org retrieved 27 Jan, 2010.
17. Johnson, Paul. 2005. *A History of the Jews.* 2nd Ed. Harper Perennial Publishers, New York, New York. p 55.
18. Johnson, Paul. 2005. *A History of the Jews.* 2nd Ed. Harper Perennial Publishers, New York, New York. P 56
19. Bratcher, Dennis. 2009. CRI/Voice Institute. *Israelite Kings.* Retrieved February 6,
20. 2010 from http://www.crivoice.org/israelitekings.html.
21. This chart is based on the chronology of John Bright *A History of Israel*, 3rd edition, Westminster, 1981.

Chapter 5
22. Hooker, Richard. 1996. The Assyrians. Retrieved 15 March, 2010 from http://www.wsu.edu:8080/~dee/MESO/ASSYRIA.HTM .
23. Retrieved March 15, 2010 from http://en.wikipedia.org/wiki/Siege.
24. Maxey, Al. (n.d.). The Silent Centuries. *Alexander the Great.* Retrieved March 22, 2010 from http://www.zianet.com/maxey/Inter2.htm.
25. Pelaia, Ariela. (n.d.) About.com Judaism. *What is Hanukkah?* Retrieved March 14, 2010 from http://judaism.about.com/od/chanukah/a/hanukkahstory.htm).

Chapter 6
26. Maxey, Al. (n.d.). The Silent Centuries. *Alexander the Great.* Retrieved March 22, 2010 from http://www.zianet.com/maxey/Inter2.htm.
27. Johnson, Paul. 1987. *A History of the Jews.* Harper Perrenial Publishers. New York, New York. p. 110-111.
28. Spiro, Ken Rabbi. 2001. Aish. *History Crash Course #31 Herod The Great.* Retrieved March 23, 2010 from http://www.aish.com/jl/h/48942446.html).
29. Johnson, Paul. 1987. *A History of the Jews.* Harper Perrenial Publishers, New York, New York. p. 114-115.
30. Gottheil, Richard & Ginzberg, Louis. 2002. Jewish Encyclopedia. *Archelaus.* Retrieved March 24, 2010 from

http://www.jewishencyclopedia.com/view.jsp?
artid=1729&letter=A&search=archelaus.

31. William Milwitzky, 2002. Jewish Encyclopedia. *Antipas*. Retrieved
    March 24, 2010 from
    http://www.jewishencyclopedia.com/view.jsp?artid=1597&letter=
    A#ixzz0j74YW0O8
32. Jackson, Wayne. (n.d.) The Christian Courier. *The Death of Herod the
    Great*. Retrieved March 23, 2010 from
    http://www.christiancourier.com/articles/723-matthew-2-19-20-the-
    death-of-herod-the-great).
33. Lendering, Jona. (n.d.) Livius: Articles on Ancient History.
    The House of Herod: Herod Agrippa. Retrieved March 23,
    2010 from http://www.livius.org/he-
    hg/herodians/herod_agrippa_i.html
34. Mahlon H. Smith. 1999. Retrieved March 24, 2010 from
    http://virtualreligion.net/iho/antipas_2.html)
35. Maxey, Al.(n.d.) The Silent Centuries. *The Roman Era*.
    Retrieved March 24, 2010 from
    http://www.zianet.com/maxey/Inter5.htm#Divided Kingdom.
36. Blank, Wayne. (n.d.). The Daily Bible Study. *The Herods*. Retrieved
    March 24, 2010 from http://www.keyway.ca/htm2002/herods.htm.
37. Here is the exact address to study the Messianic prophecies in the Old
    Testament. http://www.bprc.org/topics/fulfill.html.
38. Retrieved March 31, 2010 from
    http://en.wikipedia.org/wiki/Palm_Sunday

Chapter 7

39. Telushkin, Joseph. 1991. *Jewish Literacy*. NY: William Morrow and
    Co. Retrieved March 31, 2010 from
    http://www.jewishvirtuallibrary.org/jsource/Judaism/revolt.html.
40. Josephus. *The Jewish War*, p. 303.
41. Dolphin, Lambert. (n.d.) Blue Letter Bible. *The Destruction of the
    Second Temple*. Retrieved April 1, 2010 from
    http://www.templemount.org/destruct2.html.
42. Josephus, Antiquities ix, 1.2
43. Josephus. *The Jewish War,* p. 292.
44. Retrieved April 7, 2010 from http://en.wikipedia.org/wiki/Masada.
45. Vander Laan, Ray. (n.d.). That the World May Know.
    Retrieved April 5, 2010 from http://www.followtherabbi.com.
46. Zuroff, Avraham & Julian, Hana Levi. (2009). Israel National
    News.com. *Jews to Recite Rare Sun Blessing at Masada'a*

Ancient Synagogue. Retrieved April 8, 2010 from http://www.israelnationalnews.com/News/News.aspx/130732.
47. Schaalje, Jacqueline. Oct/Nov 1999. The Jewish Magazine. *Visiting Masada.* Retrieved April 7, 2010 from http://www.jewishmag.com/26mag/masada/masada.htm.
48. Fletcher, Rachel. (n.d.) Bible Lands and Cities. *Masada.* Retrieved April 7, 2010 from http://www.bible-lands.net/fortresses/masada/thezealots-last-stand).
49. Masada Literature. Retrieved April 7, 2010 from http://www.parks.org.il/BuildaGate5/general2/data_card.php?cat=~25~~736559308~Card12~&ru=&SiteName=parks&Clt=&Bur=228411689.
50. Johnson, Paul. 1987. *A History of the Jews.* Harper Perrenial Publishers. New York, New York.
51. Aelia Capitolina. Retrieved April 8, 2010 from http://www.absoluteastronomy.com/topics/Aelia_Capitolina).
52. Palestine Name Origin. Retrieved April 8, 2010 from http://www.palestinefacts.org/pf_early_palestine_name_origin.php
53. Honig, Sarah. Nov 25, 1995. *The Jerusalem Post.* Retrieved December 6, 2010 from http://www.palestinefacts.org/pf_early_palestine_name_origin.php.
54. Shneer, Aviv. Retrieved April 9, 2010 from http://www.culturaljudaism.org/pdf/ Contemplate_AvivShneer.pdf.
55. Map is mine, adapted from SpiritRestoration.org retrieved April 9, 2010 from http://www.spiritrestoration.org/Church/Research %20History%20and%20Great%20Links/Maps/Jewish%20Diaspora.gif
56. Stats found at My Jewish Learning.com (n.d.). Retrieved December 8, 2010 from http://www.myjewishlearning.com/history/ Jewish_World_Today/Jews_Around_the_Globe.shtml

Chapter 8

57. Twain, Mark. 1869. *Innocents Abroad.* Retrieved April 23, 2010 from http://cojs.org/cojswiki/Quotes_from_Pilgrims_to_the_Holy_Land.
58. Center for Online Judaic Studies. Melville, Herman quote retrieved April 23, 2010 from http://cojs.org/cojswiki/Quotes_from_Pilgrims_to_the_Holy_Land.
59. Isseroff, Ami. 2005. The Encyclopedia and Dictionary of Zionism and Israel. *Dreyfus Affair.* Retrieved April 12, 2010 from www.zionism-israel.com/dic/Dreyfus_Affair.htm).
60. American-Israeli Cooperative Enterprise. 2010. Jewish Virtual Library. *Theodore Herzl.* Retrieved April 12, 2010 from http://www.jewishvirtuallibrary.org/jsource/biography/Herzl.html.

61. Israel Ministry of Foreign Affairs. The text of the Balfour Declaration Retrieved April 12, 2010 from http://www.mfa.gov.il/MFA/Peace+Process/Guide+to+the+Peace+Process/The+Balfour+Declaration.htm

62. Israel Ministry of Foreign Affairs. 1999. *Chaim Wiseman*. Retrieved April 19, 2010 from http://www.mfa.gov.il/MFA/History/Modern%20History/Centenary%20of%20Zionism/Zionist%20Leaders-%20Chaim%20Weizmann)

63. Katz, Lisa. 2010. *3000 years of Jerusalem History: An expanding city.* Retrieved April 26, 2010 from http://judaism.about.com/library/1_jerusalem/bl_jerusalemhistory4.htm).

64. Jerusalem springing to life. Retrieved April 26, 2010 from http://jeru.huji.ac.il/ei1.htm.

65. Trueman, Chris. (n.d.). History Learning Site. Retrieved April 21, 2010 from http://www.historylearningsite.co.uk/treaty_of_versailles.htm).

66. Palestine facts.org. 2010. *British Mandate.* Retrieved April 21, 2010 from http://www.palestinefacts.org/pf_mandate_overview.php.

67. Luscomb, Steven. 1996-2010. British Empire.co.uk. Retrieved April 19, 2010 from http://www.britishempire.co.uk/maproom/palestine.htm. However at print, the page could not be confirmed as the "map room" pages were offline.

68. Palestine facts.org. 2010 . *What was the British White Paper of 1922?* Retrieved April 21, 2010 from http://www.palestinefacts.org/pf_mandate_whitepaper_1922.php.

69. The Truman Library.org provides a succinct chain of events of this time period in Israel. http://www.trumanlibrary.org/whistlestop/study collections/israel/large/index.php?action=chrono

70. Palestine Facts.org. 2010. *Why did the British oppose Jewish immigration to Palestine?* Retrieved October 28, 2010 from http://www.palestinefacts.org/pf_mandate_oppose_immigratio n.php

71. Knowlton, Tom. 2003. Free Republic. *Nazi Roots of Modern Radical Islam.* Retrieved April 26, 2010 from http://www.freerepublic.com/focus/news/816232/posts.

72. Israel Ministry of Foreign Affairs. (n.d.) UN General Assembly. Retrieved April 26, 2010 from http://www.mfa.gov.il/MFA/Peace%20Process/Guide%20to%20he%20Peace%20Process/UN%20General%20Assembly%20Resolution%20181).

73. Truman Library. (n.d.). Recognition of the State of Israel, Background. Retrieved April 26, 2010 from http://www.trumanlibrary.org/whistlestop/study_ collections/israel/large/index.php.

74. Yad Vashem. (n.d.). The Holocaust. FAQ. *What were the extermination camps? When did they start to function? And what was their purpose?* Retrieved April 27, 2010 from http://www1.yadvashem.org/yv/en/holocaust/resource_center/faq.asp
75. Israel News.net. December 5, 2010. *Israeli firefighters put out big Carmel fire.* Retrieved December 8, 2010 from http://www.israelnews.net/story/715996.

Chapter 9

76. Answering Christianity.com. (n.d.). Chart retrieved February 8, 2010 from http://www.answering-christianity.com/muhammad_family_tree.htm.
77. Osterholm, Tom. (n.d.) Sound Christian.com. *The Table of Nations and Origin of Nations.* Retrieved February 9, 2010 from http://www.soundchristian.com/man.
78. Keohane, Alan. 1994. *Bedouin, Nomads of the Desert,* Kyle Kathi Ltd., London. Retrieved Feb 9, 2010 from http://nabataea.net/12tribes.html.
79. Religion Facts.com. 2004-2010. *The Life of the Prophet Muhammad.* Retrieved Feb 11, 2010 from http://www.religionfacts.com/islam/history/prophet.htm.
80. Little, Gene. 2003. *The Mystery of Islam.* No publisher name available. ISBN # 0972497005
81. Little, 2003, p.54 *The Mystery of Islam.* No publisher name available. ISBN # 0972497005.
82. Bard, Mitchell G. *The Complete Idiot's Guide to Middle East Conflict.* 3rd Edition. NY: Alpha Books, 2005. Retrieved Feb 11, 2010 from www.jewishvirtuallibrary.org/jsource/biography/ Muhammad.html
83. Little, 2003, p.52. *The Mystery of Islam.* No publisher name available. ISBN # 0972497005
84. Little, 2003, p. 93-94. *The Mystery of Islam.* No publisher name available. ISBN # 0972497005
85. Little, 2003, p.55. *The Mystery of Islam.* No publisher name available. ISBN # 0972497005
86. Little, 2003. *The Mystery of Islam.* No publisher name available. ISBN # 0972497005

Chapter 10

87. McKay. *Against All Odds Israel Survives.* Questar Studios. 2005.
88. Map from *Palestine Under the Muslims: A Description of Syria and the Holy Land from AD 650 to 1500,* by Guy Le Strange, London 1890.

Copyright expired. Retrieved Feb 10, 2010 from http://en.wikipedia.org/wiki/Palestine#cite_ref-Sharonp4_4-1.
89. Wikipedia.com, Palestine(n.d.) Retrieved April 30, 2010 from http://en.wikipedia.org/wiki/ Palestine.
90. Peters, Joan. *From Time Immemorial.* Direct quote page numbers cited in-text.
91. (Schechtman, *Refugee in the World*, p. 248 citing Al-Hayat, June 25, 1959)
92. *Tuesday Night Live from Jerusalem*, Jan 17, 2010, Episode 38: "The Solution to the Crisis in the Middle East" retrieved Dec 15, 2010 from http://www.thelandofisrael.com/media-tv-shows

Chapter 11

93. (Herzog, *The Arab-Israeli Wars*. Revised by Shlomo Gazit, Revised 2004. p. 22,)
94. Ami Isseroff. 2008. Zionism and Israel Encyclopedic Dictionary. *Burma Road*. Retrieved April 30, 2010 from http://www.zionism-israel.com/dic/Burma_Road.htm.
95. History Central.Com.(n.d.). *A History of Israel: 1956 Sinai Campaign.* Retrieved April 30, 2010 from http://www.historycentral.com/Israel/1956SinaiCampaign.html.
96. Sixdaywar.com. 2007. *Timeline.* Retrieved April 30, 2010 from http://www.sixdaywar.co.uk/timeline-concise.htm.
97. Greenspan. *Against All Odds Israel Survives*, Questar Studios. 2005)
98. Herzog, *The Arab-Israeli Wars.* Revised by Shlomo Gazit, revised 2004. p. 195-197, 223, 239, 241-242.
99. Palestine Facts.org. 2010. *Israel 1967-1991: The Olympic Team Murders.* Retrieved May 12, 2010 from http://palestinefacts.org/pf_1967to1991_munich.php. p. 195.
100. McKay, *Against All Odds Israel Survives*, Questar Studios. 2005).
101. Retrieved May 12, 2010 from http://www.lars-klein.com/start/usa/nixon/nixon yomkippur.html
102. No author listed. http://godhistoryandyou.blog spot.com/2009/03/nixon-pastor-john-hagee-golda-meir.html March 4, 2009, no author listed
103. Lebanon War (n.d.) retrieved May 14, 2010 from http://www.jewishvirtuallibrary.org/jsource/History/Lebanon_War.html.
104. Hezbollah Prisoner Swap retrieved May 14, 2010 from http://en.wikipedia.org/wiki/2008_Israel-Hezbollah_prisoner_swap.

105. Herzog, *The Arab-Israeli Wars*. Revised by Shlomo Gazit, Revised 2004. p 430.
106. Archbold, Norma Parrish. 2008. *Green Horse: The Bible and Islam.* p. 85. This is an excellent source. She lists no publisher is my first edition copy.
107. Greenspan speaking in *Against All Odds Israel Survives*, Questar Studios. 2005.
108. Kauffman, Ami. January 27, 2012. Poll: 70% of Israeli Jews believe 'Jews are chosen people'. Retrieved February 2, 2012 from http://972mag.com/poll-shows-israel-slowly-but-surely-turning-into-a-theocracy/33989/
109. Hope For Israel Newsletter email. January 30, 2012. Published from Richmond Virginia.

Chapter 12

110. Aridi, Naim. 2002. Ministry of Foreign Affairs.gov.il *Focus on Israel—The Druze in Israel.* Retrieved May 25, 2010 from http://www.mfa.gov.il/MFA/MFAArchive/2000_2009/2002/1 2/Focus+on+Israel-+The+Druze+in+Israel.htm .
111. For more information on the Armenian Genocide see http://en.wikipedia.org/wiki/Armenian_Genocide
112. Hagopian, Arthur. 1986. Jerusalem Center for Public Affairs. *Armenians in Israel.* Retrieved May 25, 2010 from http://www.jcpa.org/jl/hit04.htm.
113. Diorio, Donna. 2009. Israel Prayer.com. *Expose. Pt 1 The Terror Bombing of Israeli Messianic Teen Ami Ortiz.* Retrieved May 31, 2010 from http://www.israelprayer.com/articles/Expose%20PT%201.html

Chapter 13

114. Vander Laan, Ray. 1995-2007. That the World May Know Ministries. *A Covenant Guarantee.* Retrieved July 21, 2010 from http://www.followtherabbi.com/Brix?pageID=3343).

Chapter 14

115. Schroeder, Gerald. (n.d.) AISH.com The Age of the universe. (para. 2) Retrieved August 14, 2010 from www.aish.com/ci/sam/48951136.html
116. Rich, Tracey. 1995-2010. Judaism 101: Jewish Calendar. Retrieved 12 January 2010 or 27th of Tevet, 5770, if you like, from http://www.jewfaq.org/calendar.htm .

117.More information on the Jewish Feasts, meanings and traditions can be found at http://www.luziusschneider.com/Papers/JewishFeasts.htm
118.Tish b' Av events with full documentation can be found at http://ohr.edu/yhiy/article.php/1088. as of Jan 25, 2010.)
119.a nice sample *Haggadah* can be reviewed at http://www.godandscience.org/apologetics/haggadah.html#QtT8T8mm NPQG
120.No author or publishing date or author affiliation is available, but the author's take is interesting. Retrieved February 21, 2010 from http://avirtualpassover.com/afikomen.htm
121.Lerner, Barry Dov. 1999-2010. About.com by New York Times. Judaism. *Why is there a cup of wine for Elijah at the Passover Seder?* Retrieved February 21, 2010 from http://judaism.about.com/od/passove1/f/elijah_why.htm.
122.Deem, Richard. 2006. Evidence For God. *How the Passover Reveals Jesus Christ.* Retrieved Feb 23, 2010 from http://www.godandscience.org/apologetics/passover.html#Gegpi1bL6Z xh)
123.MacArthur, John. 1986-1010. Retrieved Dec 15, 2010 from http://www.biblebb.com/files/mac/2382.htm,
124.Cockrill, Milbeurn. (n.d.). Bible Study.org. *Was Jesus in the Grave three days and nights?* Retrieved Feb 25, 2010 from http://www.biblestudy.org/basicart/was-jesus-in-the-grave-for-three-days-and-nights.html.

Chapter 15

125.Benner, Jeff. 1999-2007. Ancient Hebrew Research Center. *The Origin of the Hebrew Language.* Retrieved November 12, 2010 from http://www.ancient-hebrew.org/11_language.html.
126.Quote Retrieved February 12, 2010 from http://www.jafi.org.il/education/100/PEOPLE/BIOS/beliezer.html). However by December 15, 2010, the page had been removed. From the Jewish Agency for Israel's website.
127.Retrieved Feb 12, 2010 from http://en.wikipedia.org/wiki/Eliezer_Ben-Yehuda.
128.Verryt, Jacki, Ulpan student in Jerusalem 2009-2010 Personal interview. "What are your observations as a foreigner learning Hebrew for the first time?" Interview took place December 18, 2009.
129.Uittenbogaard, Arie. 2000-2010. Abarim-Publications.com. *Meaning of Sarah.* Retrieved Dec 24, 2009 http://www.abarim-publications.com/Meaning/Sarah.html.